© Verlag Zabert Sandmann, Munich, Germany 2006

© for the English edition:
Verlag Zabert Sandmann, Munich, Germany 2007
ISBN 978-3-89883-158-1

Graphic design	Barbara Markwitz, Kuni Taguchi
Cover illustration	Rupert Stöckl
Photography	Kai Stiepel (recipes),
	Dr. Kai-Uwe Nielsen (introduction)
Illustration	Frank Duffek
Recipes	Hofbräuhaus Munich, Karl Benner,
	Erhard Schneider, Marco Schön
Introduction	Jossi Loibl
Editors	Julei M. Habisreutinger,
	Martina Solter, Nicole Fischer
Production	Karin Mayer, Peter Karg-Cordes
Lithography	Christine Rühmer,
	MMintec GmbH, Miesbach
Translation	Dr. Ina Verstl, Germering
Printing and binding	L.E.G.O., Vicenza

THE Hofbräuhaus COOKBOOK

Contents

Foreword
6

The History of the Hofbräuhaus
8

The Cuisine
26

Snacks & Starters
36

Soups & Salads
50

Vegetarian & Side Dishes
64

Fish
80

Meat
92

Desserts
122

Index of Recipes
134

Foreword

Bavarian cuisine has a long tradition which dates back several centuries. Its dishes are hearty and diverse. Using predominantly local food products, they have their own distinctive character. Originally, Bavarian cuisine bore testimony to farming life. Courtly culture and genteel affluence in the cities have refined it. As the culinary manifestation of Bavarian mentality, it conveys a very special way of life.

In our fast-moving time and age, it is very important to enjoy the food that you are eating with awareness. Bavarian cuisine has always been promoting this healthy attitude to food consumption. Slowly and with reverence, each meal is being celebrated, because to enjoy a meal with all your senses is more than just eating and drinking. It shall give you pleasure – the pleasure of company, of spending time with other people. This is what we mean by Gemütlichkeit, when body and mind, heart and soul are overcome with joy.

Therefore, Bavarian cuisine is inextricably linked with Bavarian beer culture and the warm hospitality to be found in our inns.

The Munich Hofbräuhaus with its 400 year old history proudly acknowledges this tradition. Others may embrace fast food. For the Hofbräuhaus, freshness is key. Our chef only uses food products which are sourced locally like chicken and seasonal vegetables which help preserve the characteristic taste of our Bavarian specialities.

Highly conscious of quality, freshness and the origin of food products, our landlord and landlady Sperger together with their chef serve you an authentic piece of Bavarian tradition with every plate they place in front of you. Every glass of beer they offer you will be a perfect accompaniment. For more than 25 years and two generations the Sperger family has guaranteed that the Hofbräuhaus offers its guests the finest Munich traditions in gastronomy.

We are pleased that the most popular recipes of the Hofbräuhaus have been put together in this book and we think that you will find much here to tempt you. We hope that our dishes will prompt you to discover, re-discover or even re-interpret the roots of our Bavarian Heimat.

Wishing you as much fun with the recipes as we have had and „an Guadn!" Enjoy!

Dr. Michael Möller
Director Staatliches Hofbräuhaus Munich

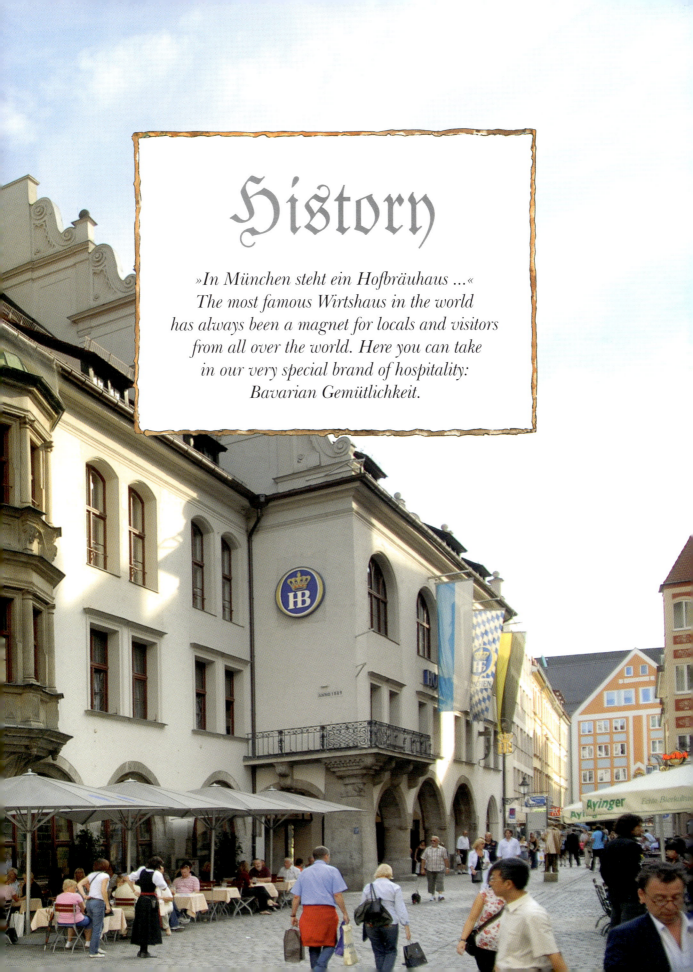

History

»In München steht ein Hofbräuhaus ...«
The most famous Wirtshaus in the world
has always been a magnet for locals and visitors
from all over the world. Here you can take
in our very special brand of hospitality:
Bavarian Gemütlichkeit.

The History
of the Most Famous Wirtshaus in the World

The founding of the Hofbräuhaus more than 400 years ago was – and still is – a real blessing for Munich's folk and visitors. However, they do not owe the most famous Wirthaus in the world to the generosity of its founder. On the contrary. Wilhelm V., who is Duke of Bavaria between 1579 and 1597, happens to be plain broke. The construction of St. Michael's Church, which he donates to the Jesuits, awards him with the epithet »the Pious«. Alas, it costs a fortune. And the upkeep of 600 courtiers does not come cheap either. The gallant ladies and noble men are constantly thirsty and they have very discriminating tastes. As they do not like the local Munich beer, the brew has to be imported from Einbeck near Hannover, several hundred miles away in the north, in wooden barrels on ox-drawn carts. Some sources claim that these beer imports amounted to 2,000 barrels per year or 130,000 liters.

Wilhelm tells his advisors to find a solution to his problem. On September 27, 1589, they reveal their ingenious plan to him: Why not build a brewery nearby, close to the court which will not require a great deal of expense? As always when it comes to making money, politicians prove highly resourceful. Wilhelm is delighted and relieved.

The same day, he hires a brewmaster for the new Hofbräuhaus who brings the project near the Residenz in today's Alter Hof to fruition. Heimeran Pongraz runs the brewery for more than twenty years, much to the pleasure of the spoilt noblemen.

Maximilian I establishes himself as an even more capable businessman than his father, whom he succeeds on the Bavarian throne. He does not only have a different taste in beer – he prefers the livelier, brighter wheat beer to the malty brown beer – he also bans all the other private breweries from brewing wheat beer, thus securing his ducal Hofbräuhaus a sizeable income. Wheat beer becomes so popular that the brewery barely manages to keep up with demand. 1,444 hectoliters of beer were brewed in 1605, which was a great amount of beer in those days. In 1607, Maximilian decides to relocate the wheat beer brewery elsewhere and

Thirst-quenching beer, a hearty fare and traditional music – a visit to the Hofbräuhaus will be a very rewarding experience.

has another brewery built at the Platzl. This is where you will find the Hofbräuhaus today. Thanks to this brewery, a lot of money finds its way into the coffers of Duke Maximilian, which he spends on financing his army during the Thirty Years' War. However, the leader of the Bavarian army cannot stop the Swedish King Gustav Adolf from conquering Munich on May 16, 1632. Only the delivery of 344 buckets (that's 22,000 liters) of bock beer saves the city from pillaging and burning. Also, 42 Munich citizens, who had been taken hostages by the Swedish, are set free.

From 1638 onwards, the much sought after May bock beer is served to Munich citizens in a shed nearby the Alte Hof, which was the Duke's Residence.

That the Hofbräuhaus at the Platzl eventually becomes a real Wirtshaus, an inn, the Munich burghers have King Ludwig I to be thankful to. His marriage to Therese of Saxony-Hildburghausen is celebrated with a fair which later is to evolve into the Oktoberfest. When several Munich brewers and landlords complain to King Ludwig I that ordinary folks increasingly manage to regale themselves with

The brothers Wolfgang (third from the left) and Michael Sperger (not in the picture), together with their chefs, offer visitors a highly original but no »stick-to-your ribs« Bavarian cuisine.

Hofbräu beer, the popular King says »rightly so«. In 1828, he decrees that beer and food are to be served at the Hofbräuhaus. This is when the Hofbräuhaus becomes open to the general public.

Johann Mayerhofer, who was present when the King is feted for his decree, notes: »(…) and when King Ludwig stood with the crowds and wrote his name above the door, everybody cried ›Hail, our king, hail‹ and the barrels in the cellars began to tremble. The Hofbräuhaus had been launched into society and the barrels had every reason to be worried.« Sixteen years later, Ludwig I again provides proof of his political instinct. On October 1, 1844, after a riot by dissatisfied soldiers, he lowers the price of a liter of Hofbräu beer to five Kreutzers from six and a half »to give the working classes and the military the opportunity to afford a healthy and inexpensive drink«. The lower price of beer makes the demand increase enormously. Regularly, the Hofbräuhaus runs empty. Almost fifty years later the royal brewery is again bursting at the seams. It is moved to Haidhausen, an area above the river Isar. At the Platzl, the Wirthaus is built in the neo-renaissance style as can be seen today. The design is by the architect Max Littmann from Chemnitz. In Munich he also builds a few more beer halls such as the Matthäser Bräusaal and the Pschorrbräu-Bierhallen, as well as the Prinzregenten Theater. He also designs the court theaters in Weimar and Stuttgart. The showpiece of the new Hofbräuhaus is the banqueting hall with its nine meter high vaulted ceiling. Its decorations of coats of arms and frescos depict personalities who shaped Bavarian and Munich history. Thanks to its size, the hall seats more than one thousand guests. Still, a total of 3,500 guests can be served simultaneously at the banqueting hall, the beer hall, the Trinkstube and the other hospitality rooms.

Since it opened its doors in 1897 the Hofbräuhaus has become a true place of pilgrimage. At the turn of the century, plenty of Munich folks went there and spent what in those times must have been a few days' wages. Celebrities come, too, for example, the Austrian

Up to 1,300 people can be seated in the beer hall under the vaulted ceiling. This is where the world meets. Wooden tabletops, where visitors have carved their initials and names, testify to this.

Empress Sisi in 1898. The vivacious Bavarian princess married the Austrian Emperor and will always be remembered best for reforming the stiff etiquette at the court in Vienna. Sadly, the good old days come to a sudden end with the outbreak of World War I. Decades of troubles are to follow. In the banqueting hall in 1919, Eugen Leviné proclaims the communist Bavarian republic and in 1920, in the same spot, Adolf Hitler his party's agenda. When Hitler's thousand-year Reich is finally destroyed, Munich lies in ruins. The Hofbräuhaus, too, has been reduced to rubbles. Only a few walls of the beer hall are still standing.

»Die Amis kommen« (the Americans are coming) everybody cried on April 30, 1945. Munich has been softened up with a bombardment, so the U.S. army does not have to force its way into the city center. Cautiously, the soldiers of the Rainbow Division march towards the town hall from the west via Pasing. In the afternoon, they arrive in Marienplatz with their army vehicles. A few ruined building to the left, they come upon the destroyed Hofbräuhaus. For the Munich citizens, the days of rubble clearing, food tickets and watery beer begin. Fortunately, the American soldiers and their dollars help to get the Munich gastronomy going again. When the soldiers are off-duty, they go drinking beer in the company of Munich »Frauleins«.

1958, right on time for Munich's 800 year anniversary, the reconstruction of today's Hofbräuhaus is completed.

For the American tourists who have come to Munich since the Fifties, a visit to the Hofbräuhaus has always been a must. Up to 30,000 people each day go to see the most famous Wirtshaus in the world. They are welcomed by the Sperger family and their staff and enjoy the refreshing beers, the delicious food and the foot-tapping music – all of which, taken together, constitute the world-renowned Gemütlichkeit. Incidentally, Gemütlichkeit does not exist in any other language – just like the Munich Hofbräuhaus, which you cannot find anywhere else except at the Munich Platzl.

Famous Guests
at the Hofbräuhaus

Such a famous and popular Wirtshaus like the Hofbräuhaus also attracts the mighty and famous. Over the past few centuries, whoever came to pay a visit to Munich did not dare walk past the Platzl without entering. This happened to the world-famous composer Wolfgang Amadeus Mozart, who in 1780 stayed in a house in nearby Burgstraße, where he put the finishing touches to his opera Idomeneo and for distraction spent many an hour at the Hofbräuhaus. His piece of work has its first night at the Munich Cuvilliés-Theater in 1781 to great acclaim.

After the re-opening in 1897, the Hofbräuhaus is a meeting place for people from many parts of the world and even more walks of life. The Austrian Empress Sisi is among them as is Wladímir Iljítsch Uljánow – also known as Lenin. Although a self-professed teetotaler, the Russian revolutionary enjoys visiting the Hofbräuhaus. For a while, the Bolshevik organizes his revolution from his flat in Schwabing, the Munich artists' quarter. As late as 1914, four years before the Russian October Revolution, he can be seen drinking at the Hofbräuhaus. The Hofbräuhaus' initials HB provide him with great delight. In Russian script they stand for NW or »Narodnaja wolja« which translates as the »people's will to freedom«. Lenin's companion Nadjeschda Krupskaja notes in her diary: »Above all, we cherish our memories of the Hofbräuhaus where the excellent beer does away with all class differences.«

Another politician, who will later enter history as the greatest mass murderer, can be seen warming up for his political agitation at the Hofbräuhaus: Adolf Hitler. While his followers take to the beer, he himself drinks mineral water only, which the landlord has to serve himself since Hitler is afraid of an assassination attempt with poison.

During the Roaring Twenties, the revue star Josephine Baker – the woman who scandalized the world by only wearing bananas on stage – is welcomed to the Platzl.

After 1945 the Hofbräuhaus, luckily, can pick up where it left off before the war. Members of the international Jet Set regularly gather at the Hofbräuhaus. The Begum Aga Khan,

The highly-popular Austrian Empress Elisabeth was a »local« Bavarian and visited the Hofbräuhaus in 1898 three months before she was assassinated by an Italian anarchist.

former Persian empress Soraya, members of the Apollo 15 crew, composer Leonard Bernstein, writer Arthur Miller, actor Arnold Schwarzenegger – the list of famous guests is seemingly endless. Most celebrities prefer to remain incognito and often succeed at it. However, if they are recognized, the rule applies: before beer, all are equal.

It is another Russian whose visit probably makes the most lasting impression on the Hofbräuhaus: Mikhail Gorbachev. The Hofbräuhaus had never seen anything like this before: standing ovations for a politician, and for a former communist to boot! Although Mr Gorbachev is no longer president of the Soviet Union when he comes to Munich in 1992 to promote his book on the collapse of communism, he is treated like the highest visitor of state. Bavaria's mountain troupes form a guard of honor; an elderly Munich citizen throws her arms around his neck and under tears thanks him for having brought peace. 15,000 wait for him at the Marienplatz. »Dear Munich people«, he begins his speech which is drowned in cheers. The evening at the Hofbräuhaus is the highlight of his visit. Unprecedented, the evening starts at 3 pm with tourists being sent away by the stewards (»No beer, Gorbachev is coming«). At 4.30 pm the banqueting hall is hopelessly overcrowded. With a delay of three hours, the Bavarian party chiefs can greet their erstwhile class enemy at their traditional fish dinner.

During his address, Gorbachev pulls out all the stops; he is charming, he is dramatic. He tells jokes about the Hofbräuhaus. With a straight face, he revives the critical events in German-Soviet relations. Everybody is standing on their seats. »Gorbi, Gorbi!«, they shout. The band plays a cossachok while a traditional Bavarian hat is placed on Mr Gorbachev's head. When people toast Mr Gorbachev and his wife Raissa, the band plays »In München steht ein Hofbräuhaus«.

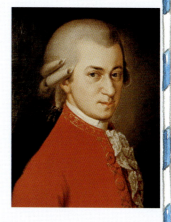

Composer Wolfgang Amadeus Mozart loved going to the Hofbräuhaus during his stay in Munich.

The Hofbräu-Hymn
and the Music in the Beer Hall

In München steht ein Hofbräuhaus, eins, zwei, gsuffa,
Da läuft so manches Fässchen aus, eins, zwei, gsuffa,
Da hat schon mancher brave Mann, eins, zwei, gsuffa,
gezeigt, was er vertragen kann, eins, zwei, gsuffa.
Schon früh am Morgen fing er an.
Und spät am Abend kam er heraus, so schön ist's im Hofbräuhaus.*

It is the hymn of all beerfully happy and a catchy tune beyond compare: the song about the Munich Hofbräuhaus. Funnily, all over the world people like to believe that this slow waltz originated in Munich and is genuine Bavarian folklore music. But no. Like the beer and the architecture of the Hofbräuhaus, the hymn is not quite as original as you might think. In fact, it is the result of very clever naturalization. The song's composer, Wiga Gabriel, was a Berliner and his music was published in Saxony. That is why in the song's very first version, it reads »eins, zwei, gsuffa« and not »oans, zwoa, gsuffa« as in the Bavarian lingo with which you may be familiar.

By the way, the song about the Hofbräuhaus initially was not even for beerdrinkers. No, it rose to prominence at the Dürkheimer Wurstmarkt, the major Palatine wine fair in 1936. There, visitors began to »schunkel« to the music, that is to rock to and fro with linked arms. In Munich, the song soon develops into the most popular sing-along of the following carnival season, thus entering into the minds and hearts of Hofbräuhaus visitors.

Records at the Hofbräuhaus relate that in those days, the band has to play »oans, zwoa, gsuffa« at least once per hour all day long. And the listeners' response is not restricted to schunkeln. Animated by beer and Gemütlichkeit, they start waltzing around – in front of the band, or even between tables and benches in the beer hall.

The tune and the rhythm are so simple and catchy that everybody can sing along – or conduct the band playing it. That's something not to be missed, decides the »Terminator« Arnold Schwarzenegger. While he is in Munich in 1998 to open a Planet Hollywood restaurant, in which he had a stake, he is seen more often at the Hofbräuhaus than at his own place across the street.

For the singer Lou Bega, a visit to the beer hall ended somewhat embarrassingly, for the onlookers rather merrily. When the bandleader spotted Lou Bega in the audience, he

* Translated Version see p. 136

quickly asked someone to bring him the sheet music of his mega hit »Mambo No 5«. When the sheets were finally stuck to the musicians' stands, they noticed to their great surprise that »Mambo No 5« was not as novel as they had thought. Its basic musical pattern stemmed from the Fifties when a wave of Latino music had swept over the country. After all, a good band does know its music. But they were in for yet more surprises. When the band approached the singer Lou Bega to ask him to join them on stage, Lou Bega had to turn down their offer. He was not allowed to sing in public because he had signed over all the rights to his agent. Not even a little serenade was to be had from Lou Bega. All he was allowed to do was to pose with the band for a television crew.

Herbert Achternbusch, a famous Bavarian poet and film director, also put in a legendary appearance when he celebrated his 60th birthday at the Hofbräuhaus. As is customary, the bandleader together with members of the band walked over to his table to play a song especially for him. Achternbusch is grumpy and greets the musicians as »beggars«, orders them about and throws a one hundred Deutschmark bill after them when they decide to beat a quick retreat. The bandleader picks up the bill and returns it to Achternbusch – after all, a Hofbräuhaus bandleader has pride, and rightly so.

Only at the Hofbräuhaus do they cherish and uphold the traditions of beer hall bands. Each day from 11 am until 3 pm as well as after 5.30 pm, a band plays from an almost limitless repertoire of Bavarian and international music in the beer hall. Of course, the song about the Hofbräuhaus is still on top of their list.

For the past few years, bands from all over Bavaria have taken the podium on weekends bringing their fan clubs with them. That way, they can make the most of a trip to Munich – and everybody will be having lots of fun.

Each day there is a band playing in the beer hall (left). In the historical banquet hall (right), Traditional Bavarian music and occasional performances of Schuhplattler dances and Goaßlschnalzer (whip cracker) provide for good entertainment.

Artists at the Hofbräuhaus
Where Original Minds Mingle

Novelists and painters, poets and draughtsmen have always liked to visit the Hofbräuhaus. It's here that they drink the beer and sample the inspiring ambience.

Popular writers like Hans von Hopfen, Karl Theodor von Heigel and Frank Wedekind were sighted at the Hofbräuhaus shortly before the turn of the 20th century. Ludwig Thoma (1867–1921), the most famous Bavarian author, already came to the Hofbräuhaus when he was still a pupil. Of his visits with his uncle, he writes in his memoirs: »When the May bock was being served, he occasionally took me with him to the Hofbräuhaus. Sometimes it happened that he fell into a dubious gaiety and on the way home placed his hat at an angle. On one of these morning visits, he pointed out to me a very old man who looked like a senior forestry official from the Jachenau or from the Königssee. ›This is Kobell‹, my uncle said. ›And now you have seen a Bavarian poet.‹«

For August Roeseler, the Hofbräuhaus is a never-ending source of motifs. Born in Hamburg, Roeseler had come to Munich to study arts. His Munich scenes were printed on postcards as well as in the satirical magazine »Flying Sheets«. He drew them all: the ill-humored waitress, the calf-knuckle eater, the tourist from Berlin, the Munich bourgeois with his dachshund.

Like Roeseler, Franz Mandlinger worked with pencil and paper. Dubbed the »Hofbräu-Rembrandt«, he rose to local prominence before World War II. He, too, had studied at the Munich Academy of Arts and wanted to travel to Italy to broaden his skills. However, in Italy a fellow student stole all his money, so that Mandlinger had to return to Munich penniless, where he tried to make a living out of drawing portraits.

The Hofbräuhaus was his hunting ground where he painted pictures of famous guests like the tenor Richard Tauber, the match box millionaire Ivar Kreuger and the American press mogul William Randolph Hearst. For payment, he was often given a beer only, or, if worst came to worst, food leftovers. When the

Left: The ceiling fresco in the staircase shows a blue sky with white clouds. They form the backdrop for several coats of arms and a crown.
Below: The porter Aloisius hard at work.

Munich bombardment reduced the Hofbräuhaus to a pile of rubble, he saw the basis of his livelihood destroyed. »Now I've got nothing left to do in this world«, he reportedly said. Four weeks before the end of the war, he was found dead in his shabby room by his neighbors.

It was literature and art which commemorate the Hofbräuhaus' most famous regular: the porter Aloisius, a fictional character created by Ludwig Thoma. Thoma chose the Hofbräuhaus in 1911 as the setting for his satire »A Municher in Heaven«. The porter Alois Hingerl works in such haste that he suffers a stroke and dies. Life in heaven does not appeal to him at all. He has to sing hosanna; for food, he only gets manna and there is no beer. When he starts to grumble over his lot, thus disrupting heavenly peace and quiet, God decides to send him back to earth with a list of divine inspirations for the Bavarian government. Alas, on his way to government house, Aloisius passes by his beloved Hofbräuhaus. On the whim of the moment, he decides to walk in to have one glass of beer, then another glass of beer and another ... and that's where he is still sitting today, while the government is waiting in vain for divine advice.

The story was published in the satirical magazine »Simplicissimus«, with illustrations by Olaf Gulbransson. During the Sixties, Aloisius made a career for himself as an animated picture character. In the Nineties, the character received a boost to his popularity when one of the contenders for the Munich mayor's office put up posters depicting himself as the angel Aloisius. Alas, the candidate first loses the elections and next the trial over breech of copyright.

Since 1999, Walter Reiner's motifs and scenes of the lovable little rotund man have adorned the Aloisius-Stüberl. Sitting there, you may feel a bit like a »Municher in Heaven«.

Beer Steins Behind Bars
The Regulars' Privilege

Those who come and sit at the regulars' table, the Stammtisch, may represent a dying breed. But not at the Hofbräuhaus. Here, this culture is still alive. At the Hofbräuhaus, the regulars find a refuge to discuss life in general and their issues in particular. From cab drivers to tennis players: the Hofbräuhaus knows of more than one hundred regulars' tables. Most of them meet once a week at the Mecca of Munich regulars, where special tables are kept for them. Above these tables, you will find signs indicating which regulars assemble here. Most regulars have their table in the beer hall. Of course, it's to see and to be seen. Definitely worth seeing are the magnificent tufts of chamois hair, the so-called Gamsbärte, reminiscent of a shaving brush, which royalists sport on their hats. Very photogenic.

The Hofbräuhaus does not promote a class society. Nevertheless, some people do enjoy privileges that others don't. And sometimes it may take decades before a regular's dream comes true: to have his own locker in one of the several wrought-iron safes, also known as the beer stein safes. People admire them, sometimes they envy them: the proud leaseholders of one of the 505 beer stein lockers. Legends have been woven around how to obtain one of these lockers. »In fact it is rather simple«, explains the landlord Wolfgang Sperger, »it is those guests who are most loyal and friendly whom we grant permission to leave their most precious possession, their stein, with us. Celebrities are not among those privileged.« The most prominent leaseholder of one of these lockers is the former director of the Hofbräu, Albert Riedl. The Munich carpenter Konrad Brunner is probably a more typical owner. Carefully, he opens the shiny brass lock, lifts the wrought-iron handle and takes out his stein with the engraved pewter lid. Ever since he received his master craftsman's diploma more than thirty years ago, he regularly has attended his Stammtisch. A few years ago, he plucked up his courage and asked the landlady Gerda Sperger if he could have one of these lockers and she promised to take

Left: There is room for 505 beer steins in the beer stein safe, one of the Hofbräuhaus' curios.
Below: When the regulars get up to leave, they rinse their steins themselves in the beer hall.

care of the matter. When the third safe was officially opened, he was one of the lucky few.

The new safe was built by the wrought-iron craftsman Manfred Bergmeister, who had already welded the first safe in 1972: »We wanted to prevent souvenir hunters from taking all our steins«, the craftsman explains. That more than thirty years later he was asked again to build a safe, is due to a contract signed then. »When the first safe was completed, the brewery and I agreed that I would not build anything similar for others – and that no one else could build a safe here except me.«

Those who have finally gotten a key will not let go of it easily. However, if a regular does not show up for extended periods of time, that is taken note of. At the end of the year, a slip of paper is placed inside the steins to remind their owners to pay their rent. Of course, there are many reasons why someone does not turn up for his regulars' table. »In most cases our guests have fallen ill. It's very tragic if they have died in the meantime«, says the landlord.

The much coveted lockers are not usually passed on to other family members, although it has happened that some descendents were allowed to take over a locker. »Of course, we do not believe in hereditary rights when it comes to own beer stein lockers. But we do talk to the family members to find out if they are really interested«, Wolfgang Sperger insists.

If you leave your stein at the Hofbräuhaus, you must have a very special relation to that stein. Many guests take it upon themselves to carry it over to the bar to have it filled with beer. They have also made it their job to cleanse it after use. When the meeting at the regulars' table is over, the participants each take their empty stein to the bar, rinse it in the big copper vat and return the stein with a large paper napkin to the safe. The napkin is placed under the lid so that it does not shut completely and air is allowed to circulate. With great care, the stein is then placed behind the wrought-iron bars – till next time.

From Einbock to May Bock

The Bock Beer Cellars

It's the year 1614. The rebuilding and furnishing of the ducal brewery at the Platzl is completed, the brews run smoothly. Still, the thirsty courtiers are displeased. Formerly they were treated with the good strong beer from Einbeck near Hannover, now they are only given the home brewed brown beer and wheat beer. They are right. The Munich beers are, in fact, less full-bodied than the beers brewed up north. So they insist on having stronger stuff, albeit locally brewed.

In 1614 Elias Pichler, who had worked in Einbeck but had been lured away in order to succeed the first Hofbräu brewmaster, Heimeran Pongraz, presents the first Munich beer brewed in Einbeck-style to the discerning noblemen. Initially, the new brew is reserved for those who sit at the Duke's table. The servants still have to drink the other, more watery beer. However, the strong dark beer soon gains so much reputation that even the Swedes, when they conquer Munich in 1632 during the Thirty Years' War, insist on receiving 22,000 liters as the victor's prize. The Munich gentry longs for the new brew to enjoy its noble taste. Elector Maximilian I eventually relents and in a side building of the Alte Hof, the »Ainpockhische«, the beer in Einbeck-style, is served to the general public for the first time. The beer is an instant success. Although the beer is only served for a short period of time during spring, demand is immense and the Hofbräuhaus has to build an extension.

Over the centuries, the name of the beer is corrupted, first to »Einbock«, later to »Bock«. Until 1818, it is the Hofbräuhaus' privilege to brew this beer, which is served in the »Old Mint« from 1826 onwards each year in May. The Munich folks soon call this location »Bockstall« or »Bockkeller«. Soldiers, politicians, civil servants, students and professors: here they all become brothers in beer. Differences of class are overcome – at least while people sit at the table. The writer and recipient of the Nobel Prize for Literature, Paul von Heyse, enthuses over the »democratizing power of beer« and praises that »(...) the lowliest worker knows that even the highest

Left: A funny postcard on the consumption of the bock beer. Below: The May bock beer is served in special glasses.

born prince or duke cannot afford a better brew than he (...).«

From 1873, the legendary beer is served at the Hofbräuhaus at the Platzl. The annual bockfest soon turns into an important social event. The »Maibockprobe«, the official first tasting of the May bock beer, becomes a "must-attend" for the big-wigs, where members of parliament and other dignitaries can indulge in the beer – for free. This is what Ludwig Thoma relates to posterity in his famous »Letters to Filser«. Of course, the politicians are not spared his acerbic wit.

The tradition of the Maibockprobe is honored to this day, although politicians and other guests do not need a Ludwig Thoma any more to poke fun of them.

Even the sharp-tongued speeches for the festive seasonal opening were top priority from 1999 to 2007. The performances of Bavaria's former Minister of Finance, Dr Kurt Faltlhauser, who recites his self-written comedy material, were legendary. Since 2008, the Turkish German comedian Django Asül provides for the humorous send-off to the Maibock season. The public interest for his German comedian style of »political satire« was so great after his first performance that the Bavarian television has already recorded and broadcasted it repeatedly. It's a good thing that the quaffable amber-colored Maibock is always available on this occasion and feeling really good you can say »Prost, schwoa'm mas obe!« (»Cheers, let's wash it all down!«).

The Brewery
Into the Future

The year 1896 represents a turning point in the history of brewing at the Hofbräuhaus. For more than 300 years, beer had been brewed right next to the Residenz. Now the brewery is to move to a site beyond the city limits to the east up on the high Isar river embankment. There, above the cellars at Innere Wiener Straße in Haidhausen, Prince Regent Luitpold orders a new brewhouse to be built. On May 22, 1896, the last brew is mashed in at the Platzl. Three weeks later, it is fermenting in the new fermenters. Equipment that is no longer used is sold as scrap metal while new installations are being bought.

On August 10, 1896, the first brew is put into the new brewhouse, which is run in accordance with modern technology and the latest findings in brewing science. Recently-invented refrigeration units are installed to allow for a better control of the brewing process. As can be expected, the beers are of a better quality and of a higher stability which is important if you want to export your beer.

In the decades to come, all Munich breweries grow in volume and hence have to relocate their production sites. The State of Bavaria, too, has to think about moving the Hofbräu brewery once more. In 1980 planning begins; in September, 1986, ground is broken at the new site in München-Riem; on November 23, 1988, the new brewery is officially opened. The project runs into 76 million Deutschmarks, that's about 38 million Euros. Having dug its own well to provide for high quality brewing water, having built new roads and laid new rail tracks as well as having purchased state-of-the-art plant and machinery, the Hofbräuhaus brewery is considered one of the most efficient breweries in Germany, if not in Europe.

The brewery's capacity was designed to be 250,000 hectoliters of beer per year. However, in order to cope with growing demand both domestically and internationally, the brewery has to be expanded seven years after coming on-stream. In August, 1995, four new lagering

Below: The drawing by G. Heine depicts the first refurbishment of the Hofbräuhaus – from a brewery to a Wirtshaus.

tanks are added to the 51 existing ones with a total capacity of over 6,000 hectoliters.

The Hofbräu brewery today produces eleven different styles of beer – from the classic Munich Helles and the traditional Dunkel to the seasonal bock and the wheat beer. All these beers please the State of Bavaria. As the brewery's sole owner, it receives a hefty dividend from the brewery each year.

The Hofbräu brewery takes great pride in Munich as its home town; the tag line »Hofbräu: Mein München« highlights it. It emphasizes the closely-knit relation between the brewery, Munich and its people. Advertising campaigns use well-known Munich scenes and motifs, peopled with Bavarian personalities in a merry mood. When it comes to beer, tradition and modernity are no contradiction. There is one immutable tenet: the Hofbräu beer will always be a Munich beer and adhere to its high standards of quality.

The letters »HB« are a well-known international label. Today, the Hofbräu brewery is engaged in direct exports, in licensing and franchising. It is not a surprise that beer lovers all over the world want the original Munich beer. As a result, renowned brewers of quality beer in the United Kingdom, in Hungary, in India and even in China were awarded a license to produce the beer locally. Of course, this requires the continuous control by the Hofbräu team.

Through its franchising agreements, the Munich institution of the Hofbräuhaus exports Bavarian Gemütlichkeit to other parts of the world. Foreign restaurateurs offer an authentic Munich Hofbräuhaus ambience to their guests. In exchange for honoring the Hofbräuhaus trademark, registered in 1879, restaurateurs receive professional support from Munich. Visitors to Las Vegas can see the result of such export agreements: in 2004, a twin Hofbräuhaus opened its doors to Las Vegas fun seekers. By the way, it is located right next to the famous Hardrock Café. In Munich, the two also face each other at the Platzl. Call this accidental?

The Cuisine

The Hofbräuhaus is open all year round. Even on Christmas Day, visitors are welcome. Thousands of liters of the very drinkable Hofbräu beer are served each year together with our traditional Bavarian specialties.

Beer

History and Pleasure

The beer that was brewed at the Hofbräuhaus in its early days would not be recognized as beer at all today, although it was produced in accordance with the Purity Law that had been issued by Duke Wilhelm IV in April 1516, to be in force in the whole of Bavaria. The Purity Law says that only barley, hops and water are allowed in beer. The key sentence of the ducal decree of 1516 reads:

»... It is our expressed intention that from now on in all our cities, our markets and our villages, only barley, hops and water shall be used for beer. Those who consciously break this law shall be punished. The legal authorities shall be entitled to confiscate the beer barrels in question as soon as they are informed of the misdemeanor and they shall show no mercy...«

The Purity Law is the oldest food regulation in the world that is still enforced today. When it was issued, it marked the high point of a century-long legal development pushed ahead by the rulers and authorities in an effort to improve the quality of beer. It ought to be remembered that in those days beer constituted the main source of nourishment. As early as 1447, the Munich councilors had demanded that brewers exclusively use barley, hops and water for brewing »... and that nothing else was allowed to be mixed into or under. Otherwise, brewers will be punished for wrongdoing.«

In the Middle Ages, brewers had proven rather ingenious when it came to adding a special flavor to their brews which would also render them less perishable. To make brown beer last longer, brewers threw in some soot. Chalk, too, was used to make beer, that had already gone sour, drinkable again. Records mention that even the highly poisonous fly mushroom served as an additive to give beer some »extra refinement«.

Up to the issuing of the Purity Law, northern German brewers had been renowned for their high quality beers as they brewed in accordance with the regulations decreed by their guilds. This was set to change with the introduction of the Bavarian Purity Law which enabled Bavarian brewers to catch up quality-wise. Nevertheless, for centuries to come, brewing was something mostly left to chance. Often brewers did not even know if fermentation would take place or not. Moreover, many brewers believed that the yeast that settles to the bottom during fermentation was a pollutant. Today, we can say with some certainty that beer in times gone by was often sour and definitely less carbonated than it is today.

The control of the brewing process, as we understand it, only became possible following the microbiological findings of Louis Pasteur, who was the first to discover the role of yeast in alcoholic fermentation.

The next pioneering work that changed the brewing process forever was the invention of the refrigerator by Carl von Linde in the late 19th century, which helped to make brewing independent from cold weather. Thanks to von Linde's refrigerators, brewers were able to produce the bright beers, the so-called »Helles«, which made Munich famous, even during the hot summer months. The Helles beer uses »bottom-fermenting« yeast which is added to the wort – that is malt dissolved in water – during fermentation. Due to the cold temperatures, the yeast gradually sinks to the bottom, unlike the »top-fermenting« yeast, which swims on top of the (wheat-)beer as temperatures are higher. Mechanical refrigeration boosted brewers' business as it allowed them to produce all styles of beer all year round – »Helles« or dark beer or stronger varieties like the »Festbier«.

Modern methods of water treatment also gave brewers a greater range of control over the brewing process. With the help of »softer« water, for example, you can brew a brighter beer, whereas water with a higher level of calcium carbonate results in beers with a darker color.

The great variety of Bavarian beers is ideal if you want to match them with your food. There are many harmonious and exciting combinations to be enjoyed. One rule applies, though: Neither food nor beer should be overpowering in flavour. They should taste good and tickle the palate.

Although one should not lay down any rules when tastes are concerned, on the pages which are to follow, you will find some recommendations as to which beers go particularly well with the authentic Bavarian dishes served at the Hofbräuhaus. Gradually but surely, brewers have begun to accept what wine connoisseurs have been saying for a long time: that the perfect mixing of beverage and food increases our pleasure no end.

Food and Drink at the Hofbräuhaus

The Bavarian cuisine is highly versatile and offers plenty of tasty treats. From a more casual snack in the beer garden while dusk is setting to a formal set meal that would delight a duke – the Hofbräuhaus caters to all tastes while maintaining its good old-fashioned affability. These are our chef's very special recommendations.

In the Beer Garden

It is one of the most cherished and fiercely defended traditions that you are allowed to bring your own food to the Munich beer gardens. On a gentle summer evening, you will see many of Munich's folks cycle to a beer garden with a hamper full of all sorts of delicatessen. For style as well as convenience, they will also bring their own tablecloths, napkins, snack boards, a big knife as well as several condiments. The extra-large pretzels, which usually come straight out of the oven, can be bought at the beer garden. The most popular cheese types are Swiss Emmental, Romadur and Tilsiter. Beer lovers often prefer sausages, for example Landjäger, Kaminwurzen and Lyoner. As we all have to eat our greens, radishes, white or red, will lie on most tables. These are the Hofbräuhaus-mouthwaterers that we would like to offer you:

Hearty favorites

Fresh Radishes, White and Red (see page 40)
Apple Lard Dripping on Fresh Rye Bread (see page 39)
Obatzda (see page 38)
Cream Cheese with Herbs (see page 46)
Munich Sausage Salad (see page 48)
Beef Salad (see page 49)

 Which beer?

In the beer garden, we usually serve our »Hofbräu Original«, a lager beer. However, the most popular is »Münchner Sommer naturtrüb«, an unfiltered bottom-fermenting lager beer which is served well-chilled. On a hot day, many guests prefer to drink a beer mix, either a »Radler-Maß« (lager with lemonade) or a »Russen-Maß« (wheat beer with lemonade).

In the Beer Hall

Whether they come from Japan, China, Australia, or the United States: the Hofbräuhaus' beer hall is the meeting place for visitors from all over the world. It only takes a Maß of beer for international understanding to get under way. Language barriers at the Hofbräuhaus? Quickly overcome. On simple wooden tables, the show-stopping Bavarian standards are served.

Our rustic Bavarian meal

Starter
Beef Consommé with Liver Dumplings
(see page 57)
Main Course
Pork Knuckle with Potato Dumpling and Cabbage Salad with Bacon (see page 100)
Dessert
Steamed Yeast Dumpling with Vanilla Custard Sauce (see page 126)

 Which beer?

According to our chef, you should have the bright »Hofbräu Original« lager beer with your starter. For the main course, he suggests that you treat yourself to a glass of »Hofbräu Dunkel«, a brown beer very rich in taste. What many people do not know is that brown beer was brewed in Bavaria long before the brighter lager beer became fashionable.

If it is cold outside, a glass of »Hofbräu Festbier« will go very well with the pork knuckle; it has slightly more alcohol and – it goes down easily.

In the Bräustüberl and the Festsaal

Those who would like to dine in style should either have their meal served in the Bräustüberl at the table inside the bay window or in the large Festsaal, our banqueting hall. Blue and white tablecloth, silver cutlery and cloth napkins help provide an aura of festive dining. The round tables are ideal for a get-together of parties of four or six who seriously love food and a good schmooze.

The Duke's menu

Starter
Beef Aspic (see page 42) or
Beef Consommé with Strips of Crepes
(see page 58)
Main Course
Beef Roulade with Potato Puree and Season's Salad (see page 108)
Dessert
Bavarian Cream with Fresh Fruit
(see page 130)

 Which beer?

Since there are several courses to follow, the festive party may be well advised to start out with a glass of fine »Hofbräu Original« as an aperitif. This beer would also be an exellent choice to accompany the first two courses. If you would like to indulge yourself with something very special for a particular celebration, ask for a glass of »Hofbräu Festbier« in winter or for a glass of »Hofbräu Maibock« in spring. These beers are real treats.

Brezn, Weißwürst, Leberkäs

The Essentials of a Munich »Brotzeit«

Plenty of guests – although they would never admit it – do not come to the Hofbräuhaus because of the beer but to have a Brotzeit, a light meal that is served all day. Brotzeit translates as »bread time«, although the bread in question usually is a pretzel or Breze (the Bavarian variety). The origins of the brown plaited bread are somewhat hazy and we shall probably never find out. One story goes like this: In 1839 a royal envoy, Wilhelm Eugen von Ursingen, visited Munich. As usual, he would order breakfast at the coffee house in Residenzstraße, which was owned by Johann Eilles, a purveyor to the royal court. Alas, the apprentice who was to prepare the Breze made a mistake. Instead of glazing the Breze with sugar he dunked it in caustic soda water ...

Today's Brezen are made from wheat. They are often sold unbaked to the restaurants so that chefs can put them into the oven as demand dictates. That way they can offer freshly baked Brezen all day round: dark brown in color, cracked open in parts, crusty but not too hard and smelling oh so temptingly!

A Breze cannot come without a »Münchner Weißwurst«, the famous white unsmoked sausage, which was invented one hundred and fifty years ago. According to popular lore, it happened on carnival Sunday February 22, 1857 in an inn called »The Sanctuary Lamp« which was located at Marienplatz, a few meters away from the Hofbräuhaus. Early in the morning, the landlord Sepp Moser had begun preparing sausages in order to be able to offer his guests very fresh veal sausages for which his inn was famous. However, when it came to filling the mince into the skins, Moser was shocked to realize that no mutton skins were left which, in those days, were used for frying sausages. And his inn was already packed out ...

In his desperation, he began filling the mince into pork skins. As they are wider in diameter and thinner, the landlord only dared boil the sausages in hot water. The new invention was greeted enthusiastically by his guests.

While Munich has agreed on this story to mark the origin of the Weißwurst, there is still a battle brewing over the correct way of eating it. Aesthetes insist on cutting the sausage, whereas purists demand the Weißwurst to be sucked empty. Adherents to the latter tech-

The definitive Bavarian Brotzeit that you can still enjoy at the Hofbräuhaus today must include all of the following: freshly tapped beer, Weißwürste (that must be eaten before the noon hour is rung), spicy hot radish and crusty Brezen.

nique seem to drop in numbers as the sausages, following the Zeitgeist and consumers' tastes, have become more and more compact, thus preventing an appreciative sucking.

For us at the Hofbräuhaus, it is a question of honor to prepare our own Weißwürste. From 4 am on, four butchers are hard at work in our butcher's shop in the vaulted cellars to produce 700 kilograms of sausages each day. If strung together, our annual sausage production would reach from Munich to Manhattan: 2,790 kilometers of pork sausages, 2,000 kilometers of white sausages, 880 kilometers of succulent roast sausages, 500 kilometers of Regensburger sausages and 390 kilometers of Wiener sausages.

Not included is the daily production of 100 kilograms of Leberkäse (liver cheese), which, by the way, contains neither liver nor cheese. The first part of its name is derived from its shape. It looks like a »Loabe« (loaf) which was corrupted to »Leber«, while »Kas« (cheese) in the Bavarian dialect refers to any kind of ground meat. Liver cheese is made from pork, beef, bacon and spices. It is usually baked in large tins in the oven. The loaf is then cut into thick slices and served in portions. Yet, at the Hofbräuhaus, we decided against the large tins and only bake small loafs so that each guest is served his own little Leberkäse, which makes the dish more appetizing.

Mustard always goes with it. Munich folks prefer to have their Leberkäse with sweet mustard. When it comes to Weißwurst, they will only accept sweet mustard. Like Breze and Leberkäse, sweet mustard was invented in Munich. Today's recipe was formulated by Johann Conrad Develey in his mustard shop in Kaufingerstraße, where in 1845 he boiled a mixture of mild mustard seeds, vinegar, sugar and spices. Before that, sugar had never been used in mustard. The way to caramelize it was with the help of a blazing-hot poker. In 1874 Johann Conrad Develey became a purveyor to the royal court. To this day, the company that bears his name delivers its famous mustard to the Hofbräuhaus.

The Heart and Soul of the Hofbräuhaus

Interview with Stilla Weiß, who has been working at the Hofbräuhaus for more than forty years

Mrs Weiß, do you remember which job you first held when you joined the Hofbräuhaus?
Mrs Weiß (laughs): Oh, that was such a long time ago. I started out in 1962 as a »Salad Dresser«. I made sure that individual salads were fresh and appetizing when served. In those days the Hofbräuhaus' kitchen also was the caterer for the Bavarian Parliament.

For many years now you have been a housekeeper at the Hofbräuhaus. Can you please tell us what your responsibilities are?
Mrs Weiß: I look after many things. For example, that there are clean table cloths, that the seasonal menus are to be found on the tables and that tables are decorated nicely. Besides, I am also in charge of maintaining stocks and cleanliness in general. I am the contact person for kitchen staff as well as for our waitresses and waiters. Formerly, when we still had our old billing system, I also had to check the till after work.

Does that mean you are the link between the kitchen and other departments?
Mrs Weiß: I think you can put it like that. Everybody who has a problem or would like to discuss something with me can come and see me. It is then my job to talk these things over with the chef or the landlord.

As the heart and soul of the house, you surely must have helped solve a few disputes and prevent trouble.
Frau Weiß: Occasionally, yes. For example, if there are busy times and someone in the kitchen is a bit of a slow worker, then I make sure I give him something else to do while I find someone who works faster. Or if a dish has not been set correctly on a plate, I decide that it shall be returned and set anew. That's what I take great care of.

How have the eating habits changed over the years?
Mrs Weiß: Years ago people used to eat heartier meals. Larger portions, less fish, hardly any vegetables or salads. Our menu was much shorter than it is today. We offered Brezen, a few meat courses and radishes which the »radish women«, the traditional Munich sales-

To always remain friendly and make sure that everything runs smoothly despite the hustle and bustle of up to 30,000 guests each day, that is the forte of the Hofbräuhaus and its employees, like housekeeper Stilla Weiß.

women of that vegetable, sold inside the Hofbräuhaus. Guests ordered what they could afford. In fact, they created their own dishes. And they drank more.

How much beer did guests use to drink at the Hofbräuhaus?

Mrs Weiß (laughs): Well, on occasion five to ten liters of beer. Today, on average, guests consume one or two liters of beer. Our regulars used to get their beer themselves at the bar and, when they were finished, they would rinse their steins in a copper vat.

When were the glass mugs – beside steins – first used at the Hofbräuhaus?

Mrs Weiß: The glass mugs were introduced in 1972 during the Munich Olympic Games. That year, a pressure group was founded to fight fraudulent serving. With glass, you see right away how much beer you have got.

Is it true that since the Olympic Games more and more tourists have been coming to the Hofbräuhaus?

Mrs Weiß: Yes, that's true. Ever since the Hofbräuhaus square was revamped, a lot more Munich people have come to the Hofbräuhaus, too.

Which dishes are most popular with foreign visitors?

Mrs Weiß: On the whole, they prefer to try our authentic Bavarian dishes. That is why we have special set menus for them. How should Chinese, Japanese or Indian visitors know that potato dumplings and cabbage are the best side dishes for a traditional pork roast?

Do you remember anything special out of these fourty years of the Hofbräuhaus?

Mrs Weiß: Oh dear, so much has happened over the years and my memory does not serve me well any longer. But I do remember well that Franz Josef Strauß, a famous Bavarian politician, always wanted to have the crispy cut end of the Leberkäse.

Don't you find your work as housekeeper much too strenuous now?

Mrs Weiß: Certainly not. I only work two days per week now. That's a work load I can easily cope with. Also, I enjoy doing my job. If possible I would like to continue working here for many years to come. Who has a job with as much atmosphere and music as I have? Music puts everybody into a good mood – our guests above all, but also all who work at the Hofbräuhaus.

Mrs Weiß, thank you for your time.

Snacks & Starters

Snack time is the best time of all. In the morning, in the evening, or any time in between there are plenty of opportunities for snacking. Moreover, the delicious nibbles might get you into the mood for a proper meal!

Obatzda
with Chives and Onion Rings

Serves 4

1 small onion

1 pound mature Brie or Camembert

2 tablespoons soft butter

1 tablespoon beer

3 tablespoons cream cheese

1 teaspoon paprika and 1 teaspoon ground cumin

white pepper, salt

½ bunch chives

1 Peel the onion and cut it in half. Chop one half finely. Cut the other half into fine half-moon shapes.

2 With a fork soften the Brie or the Camembert in a small bowl. Add the butter, the beer and the cream cheese and mix well.

3 Add the chopped onion and season the mix with paprika, cumin, salt and pepper. Cover the Obatzda and keep refrigerated for one hour.

4 Wash the chives, shake them dry, and cut into fine rolls. Scoop the Obatzda onto plates and garnish with chives and sliced onion. Serve with bread or Brezen fresh from the oven.

Our chef suggests:

You can also prepare the Obatzda with left-over cheese. If you have very young Camembert, you can mash it up with a few tablespoons of cream. By the way, »Obatzda« in Bavarian means »dressed up« or »mixed«. However, the name derives from the expression »obazn« which originally meant to soil your clothes with food.

Snacks

Apfelgriebenschmalz
Apple Lard Dripping on Fresh Rye Bread

Serves 4

1 pound raw pork fat (from the belly)

2 onions

1-2 cloves garlic

1 large slightly tart apple (e.g. Braeburn)

1 tablespoon dried marjoram

3 white peppercorns

1 bay leaf

salt

4 slices of fresh rye bread

1 Dice the pork fat into small cubes, add to a saucepan and render over medium heat, occasionally stirring, until the greaves have been reduced to the size you want.

2 Peel the onions and the garlic and dice finely. Peel the apple, quarter and core it. Cut the quarters crosswise into fine slices.

3 Add the onions, garlic and apples to the dripping. Season with marjoram, peppercorns, bay leave and salt. Allow to simmer until the onions are slightly golden.

4 Remove the bay leaf. Fill the dripping into small earthenware pots. Keep refrigerated for several hours.

5 When the dripping has turned solid, remove it from the fridge and spread it on fresh rye bread.

Our chef suggests:

When rendering pork fat, the final drippings should have a bright yellow color and still have some fat to them. When frying »Röstkartoffeln« (see page 70) or »Kartoffelschmarrn« (see page 71) you can use dripping instead of bacon.

Snacks

Frischer Radi
Fresh Radishes with Chives on Bread

Serves 4
4 white radishes
2 bunches red radishes
salt
1 bunch chives
4 slices of rye bread
butter

1 Trim and wash the radishes. Peel the white radishes. Rub the red radishes dry.

2 Cut the white radishes crosswise into thin slices but take care not to cut the slices right through. Salt the slices and leave to sweat.

3 Wash the chives, shake dry and cut into fine rolls.

4 Butter the slices of bread and sprinkle with chives. Quarter the slices of bread to taste.

5 Place the white radishes on wooden plates together with the red radishes and the bread and serve.

Our chef suggests:

Always use a very sharp knife to cut the radish.
Cut right-angle gashes into the radish.
Then turn around the radish and cut slanted gashes.
That way the radish can be pulled wide like
an accordion.

Snacks

Tafelspitzsülze
Beef Aspic with Crème Fraîche

Serves 4

For the aspic jelly:

10 ounces braised beef

1 small leek

1 carrot

2-3 ounces celeriac

2 bunches chives

6 leaves gelatin

½ quart beef consommé (for recipe see page 52)

For the crème fraîche with herbs:

4 ounces crème fraîche or thick sour cream

4 tablespoons freshly chopped herbs

(e.g. parsley, chives, dill)

salt

1 To prepare the aspic jelly, cut the beef into thin slices. Trim and wash the leak. Cut into fine rings. Wash and peel the carrot and the celeriac. Dice finely.

2 Boil the vegetables briefly in hot water. Chill in ice water. Drain in a colander and set aside. Wash the chives, shake dry and cut into fine rolls.

3 Soak the gelatin in cold water until soft and squeeze dry. Heat the beef consommé in a saucepan. Add the gelatin and allow to dissolve. Remove the stock from the heat. Leave to cool.

4 Shortly before the stock turns to jelly, line the bottom of a rectangular tin with foil. Fill the tin with half of the sliced beef, half of the vegetables and half of the chives. Pour over half of the liquid. Leave the jelly to cool.

5 When it is almost set, add the remaining beef, the vegetables and the chives and pour over the remaining liquid. Cover the jelly with foil and keep refrigerated over night. Allow to set completely.

6 The following day place the tin briefly into hot water. Loosen the jelly from the tin with a sharp knife and turn out onto a platter. Remove the foil and cut the jelly into half inch thick slices. Place two slices onto each plate.

7 Whisk the crème fraîche in a small bowl, add the herbs and season with salt. Serve the beef aspic with the creme fraîche, some lettuce, bread or Brezen.

Snacks

Kartoffelkas
Potato Spread with Sour Cream

Serves 4
1 pound mealy potatoes
salt
1 medium-sized onion
½ cup cream
½ cup sour cream or crème fraîche
freshly ground pepper
freshly ground nutmeg

1 Boil the potatoes in salted water for 20 to 25 minutes until soft. Drain and leave to cool briefly. Peel the potatoes and press them through a potato press (alternatively a colander) into a bowl.

2 Peel the onions and dice finely. Add the cream and the sour cream to the potatoes and mix until smooth.

3 Add the chopped onions and season the potato spread with salt, pepper and nutmeg. Keep refrigerated for one hour.

4 Spread the potato-cream mix generously on rye bread. Garnish with chopped chives or parsley, red radishes, onion rings and serve on wooden plates.

Our chef suggests:

Should the potato spread be too dense after cooling, you can add more cream or sour cream until it becomes easier to spread. The potato spread tastes best when it is made fresh.

Geräuchertes Forellenfilet
Smoked Trout Fillet with Horseradish

Serves 4

2-3 inches horseradish

5 ounces cream

salt

sugar

lettuce

8 slices of toast

4 1/2 ounces butter

8 smoked trout fillets

4 slices lemon

4 slices cucumber

1 Wash and peel the horseradish. Grate finely. Whip the cream and add the horseradish. Season with salt and sugar.

2 Wash the lettuce and shake dry. Break up the leaves. Toast the bread and butter it generously.

3 Place the trout fillets on plates, two each.

4 Garnish with lettuce, horseradish, lemon and cucumber slices and serve with toast.

Snacks

Räucherfischmousse
Smoked Fish Mousse with Lettuce

Serves 4

For the mousse:

*1 pound smoked fish
(e.g. cod, mackerel, plaice
or herring)*

2 shallots

1 bunch dill

1 lemon

5 ounces crème fraîche

salt

freshly ground pepper

For the salad:

1 lettuce or endive

1 tomato

2 tablespoons white wine vinegar

sugar, 1 teaspoon mustard

6 tablespoons olive oil

1 Skin the fish and remove the bones. Break the fish into small pieces.

2 Peel the shallots and dice them finely. Wash the dill, shake dry, pluck the tips and chop finely. Squeeze the lemon.

3 In a tall mixing bowl, combine the fish, the crème fraîche, half of the shallots and the chopped dill. Add half of the lemon juice and mix together with a blender until smooth. Pour the mousse into a bowl and keep refrigerated for one hour.

4 Wash the lettuce and shake dry. To peel the tomato, make an X with a sharp knife on the bottom, dip it into boiling water for 1 minute, remove the tomato and set aside to cool. Peel, de-seed and dice.

5 For the salad dressing, season the vinegar and the remaining lemon juice with salt, pepper and a pinch of sugar. Add mustard and oil. Mix under the tomatoes and the remaining shallots. Before serving, pour the dressing over the lettuce and mix well.

6 Remove the smoked fish mousse from the fridge and scoop small servings of mousse onto plates. Garnish with salad and serve.

Snacks

Kräuterfrischkäse
Cream Cheese with Herbs Served in Red Pepper

Serves 4

2 red bell peppers

½ bunch each parsley, chervil, thyme, basil, dill, chives

1 pound cream cheese

salt

freshly ground pepper

4 tablespoons paprika

sugar

1 Cut the peppers lengthwise, de-seed and wash.

2 Wash the herbs and shake dry. Pluck the leaves, reserve some for garnishing. Chop the rest finely. Cut chives into fine rolls.

3 Mix the herbs and the cheese in a bowl. Season with salt, pepper, paprika and two pinches of sugar.

4 Divide the cheese mix among the four red pepper halves and garnish with herb leaves.

5 Place the stuffed red pepper halves on wooden plates and serve with a slice of rye bread or Brezen.

Our chef suggests:

Instead of cream cheese, you can also use ricotta or cottage cheese. Horseradish provides the cheese with a very special flavor. However, you can also add finely diced olives or capers to the cheese.

Snacks

Münchner Wurstsalat
Munich Sausage Salad with Onion Rings

Serves 4

2 onions

8 Regensburger sausages (alternatively 1 pound ham sausage or bologna)

2 gherkins

4 tablespoons white wine vinegar

salt

freshly ground pepper

6 tablespoons oil

1 bunch chives

1 Peel the onions and cut into fine rings. To peel the sausages, make a shallow cut lengthwise and peel off the skin. Cut into thin slices. Cut the gherkins lengthwise into thin slices so that they spread out like a fan.

2 For the salad dressing, season the vinegar with salt and pepper. Whisk in the oil. Wash the chives, shake dry and reserve a few stems for garnishing. Cut the rest into fine rolls.

3 Arrange the sausages in overlapping slices around the complete outer rim of the plate. Continue in this fashion until the plate is covered. Sprinkle with onion rings and salad dressing. Leave to marinate briefly, then garnish with gherkins and chives. Serve with rye or sourdough bread.

Rindfleischsalat

Beef Salad with White Mushrooms

Serves 4

1 pound braised beef
1 large onion
3 gherkins
1 large carrot
1 red pepper
4 ounces white mushrooms
1 large apple
1 bunch parsley
6 tablespoons gherkin pickle
6 tablespoons oil
1 teaspoon Worcester Sauce
garlic salt
freshly ground pepper

1 Cut the braised beef into half inch thick slices, then dice into thumb-sized cubes. Peel the onion and cut into fine rings. Cut the gherkins lengthwise into slices.

2 Peel the carrot and cut into circles. Cut the red pepper into half. Core, de-seed and wash. Cut into thin strips.

3 Rub the mushrooms clean and cut into quarters. Peel the apple, quarter and core. Cut into thin slices and briefly dip them into cold salted water so that they do not turn brown.

4 Add all the ingredients to a large bowl. Wash the parsley, shake dry, pluck the leaves and chop finely.

5 For the salad dressing, season the gherkin pickle with oil, Worcester Sauce, one pinch of garlic salt, pepper and add the parsley. Mix the salad with the dressing and leave to marinate for one hour. Season with salt and pepper before serving.

Our chef suggests:

Add some medium-hot mustard or pumpkin seed oil and the salad will taste even nicer. You can serve it with fried potatoes or a slice of rye bread.

Soups & Salads

Bavarian cuisine centers on good beef consommé. The clear bouillon is the basis for most Bavarian soups. Grits dumplings, liver dumplings and strips of crepes are all served in a beef consommé. And don't forget: it gives the Bavarian potato salad its typical taste.

Klare Rinderbrühe
Beef Consommé

Serves 8
1 pound beef bones
½ onion
2 small carrots
4 ounces celeriac
1 small leek
1 bunch parsley
2-3 sprigs of lovage
1 bay leaf
allspice
freshly ground nutmeg
salt
freshly ground pepper

1 Wash the bones. Boil them briefly in hot water. Drain in a colander and set aside.

2 Wash the onion and cut in half. In a large saucepan fry the onion halves until golden.

3 Add 2 ½ quarts cold water, the bones and bring to the boil. Skim off any scum from the surface. Cover and allow to simmer for 4 hours.

4 Trim and peel the carrots and the celeriac. Trim and wash the leek. Chop the vegetables coarsely. Wash the parsley and lovage and shake dry.

5 Add the vegetables, the parsley, the lovage, the bay leaf and 1 pinch each of allspice and nutmeg to the stock and season with salt and pepper. Allow the stock to simmer for another 45 minutes.

6 Strain the stock through a very fine sieve without forcing and allow to cool completely. Skim and keep refrigerated.

Our chef suggests:

*This is the fundamental, pure and essential beef consommé
and it tastes better than anything that you can buy.
To make preparing it worth your time, double the volumes.
The consommé serves plenty of uses. If you pour it into ice cube trays,
it can be stored in the freezer. For an even heartier consommé,
you might like to add a pound of beef.*

Bayerische Kartoffelsuppe
Bavarian Potato Soup with Bacon

Serves 4

2 large onions

5 ounces streaky smoked bacon

1 pound mealy potatoes

1 carrot

3 ounces celeriac

1 small leek

1 clove garlic

4 ounces butter

1 ½ quarts beef consommé (see page 52)

½ teaspoon dried marjoram

½ teaspoon dried thyme

salt, freshly ground pepper

freshly ground nutmeg

½ bunch parsley

1 Peel the onions and dice finely. Dice the bacon into small cubes.

2 Wash and peel the potatoes, the carrot and the celeriac and dice finely. Trim and wash the leek and cut into rings. Peel the garlic.

3 Melt the butter in a large saucepan and fry the onions and the bacon until golden. Add the potatoes, the carrot, the celeriac and the leek and fry briefly.

4 Add the beef consommé and the dried herbs. Season the potato soup with salt, pepper and 1 pinch of nutmeg and allow to simmer for 20 minutes.

5 For a smoother soup, you can use a blender. Season with salt and pepper.

6 Wash the parsley and shake dry. Pluck the leaves and chop finely. Sprinkle the potato soup with parsley and serve.

Soups & Salads

Gulaschsuppe
Goulash Soup with Diced Potatoes

Serves 4

½ pound beef (from the shoulder)

2 large onions

1 clove garlic

3 tablespoons oil

2 teaspoons tomato paste

2 tablespoons paprika

2 ¼ quarts beef consommé (see page 52)

½ teaspoon dried marjoram

1 teaspoon grated lemon rind

½ teaspoon ground cumin

salt

freshly ground pepper

2 waxy potatoes

½ red pepper

1 teaspoon butter

1 teaspoon flour

1 Wash the beef, dab dry and cut into small cubes. Peel the onions and the garlic and chop finely.

2 Heat the oil in a large saucepan and fry the onions and the garlic until golden. Add the beef and fry until the meat juices have been reduced.

3 Mix under the tomato paste and the paprika and fry briefly.

4 Add the beef consommé, the marjoram, the lemon rind and the cumin and season with salt and pepper. Bring to the boil. Cover and allow to simmer for 75 minutes until the meat is tender.

5 Peel the potatoes and dice finely. Cut the pepper into half, de-seed and wash. Dice finely. Mix the butter and the flour into a small ball and knead well.

6 Add the potatoes and the pepper to the soup and allow to simmer for 20 minutes. Add the butter-flour mix to the soup in morsels to thicken.

7 Season the goulash soup with salt and pepper. Garnish with fresh marjoram leaves. Serve with white or rye bread.

Soups & Salads

Grießnockerlsuppe
Beef Consommé with Grits Dumplings

Serves 4
2 ounces soft butter
3 ounces wheat grits
1 egg
salt
freshly ground nutmeg
1 quart beef consommé (see page 52)
½ bunch chives

1 Whisk the soft butter in a bowl until fluffy. Whisk in one tablespoon of grits.

2 Whisk in the egg, the remaining grits, some salt and 1 pinch of nutmeg. Set aside and allow to swell for 20 minutes.

3 Heat the beef consommé in a saucepan.

4 Dip two tablespoons into cold water each time before scooping out the grits dumplings. Immediately add the dumplings to the consommé and allow to boil for 5 minutes.

5 Reduce the heat and allow the grits dumplings to simmer for 15 minutes until done.

6 Wash the chives and shake dry. Cut into fine rolls. Place the grits dumplings into soup plates, add some consommé, sprinkle with chives and serve.

Leberknödelsuppe
Beef Consommé with Liver Dumplings and Fresh Marjoram

Serves 4

4 1/2 ounces stale hard bread rolls, cut into thin slices

8 tablespoons lukewarm milk

1 small onion

1 tablespoon butter

1/2 bunch parsley

3 sprigs of marjoram

1/2 bunch chives

1/2 pound ground beef liver

1 egg

salt

freshly ground pepper

breadcrumbs

1 quart beef consommé (see page 52)

1 Add the bread roll slices to a bowl, pour over the lukewarm milk, cover and allow to rest for 30 minutes.

2 Peel the onion and chop finely. Melt the butter in a pan and fry the onions until golden.

3 Wash the parsley, the marjoram and the chives and shake dry. Pluck the leaves and chop finely. Cut the chives into fine rolls.

4 Add the onions, the herbs, the ground liver and the egg to the bread mix and whisk. Season with salt and pepper. Should the dumpling-mix be too runny, add 1 to 2 tablespoons of breadcrumbs.

5 Heat the beef consommé in a saucepan.

6 Moisten your hands, shape small dumplings, add to the consommé and allow to simmer for 15 minutes until done. Larger dumplings may take 25 minutes.

Our chef suggests:

If you do not have enough stale hard bread rolls, use stale French or Italian bread instead.

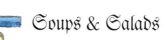

Pfannkuchensuppe
Beef Consommé with Strips of Crepes

Serves 4

1 ½ cups all-purpose flour
2 eggs
1 cup milk
salt
freshly ground pepper
freshly ground nutmeg
2 tablespoons butter
1 quart beef consommé (see page 52)
¼ bunch parsley

1 Sift the flour into a bowl and whisk in the eggs and the milk.

2 Season with salt, pepper and nutmeg. Allow the crepe-mix to swell for 15 minutes.

3 Bake thin crepes in a buttered non-stick pan. Allow to cool. When cold, roll up the crepes and cut into thin slices.

4 Heat the beef consommé in a saucepan. Wash the parsley and shake dry. Pluck the leaves and chop finely.

5 Place the strips into four soup plates, pour over the beef consommé and sprinkle with parsley before serving.

Our chef suggests:

If you like, you can add the parsley to the crepe mix. That does not only look better, it also tastes better. Crepes can be made in advance and stored in the freezer, so you will always have the major ingredient to this delicious soup ready at hand!

Soups & Salads

Rettichsalat
Radish Salad with Watercress

Serves 4
1 pound white or red radish
salt
2 tablespoons vinegar
2 tablespoons oil
freshly ground pepper
watercress

1 Trim and peel the radish and cut into thin slices. Alternatively, you can shred the radish finely on a grater.

2 Add the radish to a bowl and season with salt. Allow to sweat for 10 minutes, then drain.

3 Pour over the vinegar and oil and season with salt and pepper. Wash the watercress and drain well. Mix the watercress under the salad or sprinkle over the salad before serving.

Our chef suggests:

Those who like their radish spicy hot do not let it »cry«, that is make it sweat with salt so that it draws water. Instead, cut the radish into thin slices, mix them with the salad dressing and serve immediately. Also, radish tastes nice with a yogurt dressing. Fold 2 to 3 tablespoons of yogurt or sour cream into the salad dressing before serving.

Soups & Salads

Krautsalat
Cabbage Salad with Bacon

Serves 4
2 pounds cabbage
salt
4 ounces streaky smoked bacon
4 tablespoons oil
3 tablespoons white wine vinegar
1 teaspoon beef extract
½ tablespoon cumin
freshly ground white pepper

1 Remove the discolored leaves from the cabbage, quarter and cut out the stalk.

2 Cut the quarters into fine strips. Alternatively, you can shred the cabbage finely on a grater. Add the cabbage to a bowl, season with salt and allow to rest.

3 Trim the bacon and dice into small cubes.

4 Heat 1 tablespoon of oil in a pan and fry the bacon cubes until they are crispy.

5 Add the bacon cubes and the oil to the cabbage. To prepare the salad dressing, mix the vinegar, the beef extract, the cumin and the remaining oil. Add to the cabbage salad and mix well. Season with salt and pepper and allow to marinate for 60 minutes. Season the cabbage salad with salt and pepper and serve.

Our chef suggests:

Instead of uncooked cabbage you can also use boiled cabbage. Shred and boil in salted water for a few minutes, drain and mix with the salad dressing as described above.

Soups & Salads

Kartoffelsalat
Potato Salad with Cucumber

Serves 4

2 pounds waxy potatoes

1 large onion

5 tablespoons oil

¾ cup beef consommé (see page 52)

4 tablespoons vinegar

1 tablespoon medium-hot mustard

salt

freshly ground pepper

½ cucumber

1 Wash the potatoes and boil for 20 minutes until soft.

2 Drain and peel while still warm and cut into slices. Add to a large bowl.

3 Peel the onion and dice finely. Heat one tablespoon of oil in a saucepan and fry the onion until transparent.

4 Add the beef consommé and remove the saucepan from the heat. Add the vinegar, the remaining oil and the mustard and pour the dressing over the warm potatoes. Season with salt and pepper and allow the salad to cool.

5 Peel the cucumber and shred finely using a grater.

6 Season the salad to taste with salt and pepper and fold in the cucumber slices. If necessary add some more dressing. The salad is supposed to be »juicy«. Garnish with chives or parsley.

Soups & Salads

Rote-Bete-Salat
Beetroot Salad with Yogurt Dressing

Serves 4
1 ¾ pounds fresh beets
salt
10 ounces plain yogurt
3 tablespoons oil
2 teaspoons lemon juice
freshly ground white pepper
sugar
½ bunch parsley

1 Wash the beets and take care not to injure their skins so that they do not drain their color and juices while boiling.

2 Place the beets inside a steaming rack and steam them over salted water for one hour until they are soft. Briefly dip them into ice water, then drain and peel them. Cut into thin slices or shred finely using a grater.

3 Add the yogurt to a bowl and whisk in the oil and the lemon juice. Season the salad dressing with salt, pepper and sugar.

4 Pour the dressing over the beets and allow to marinate for 15 minutes.

5 Wash the parsley and shake dry. Pluck the leaves and chop finely. Sprinkle the salad with chopped parsley and serve.

Our chef suggests:

*As the juice of the boiled beets will tint your hands,
wear disposable gloves when you peel them.
This salad can be prepared well in advance
and will keep refrigerated for several days.
You can also season the salad with capers cut in half.*

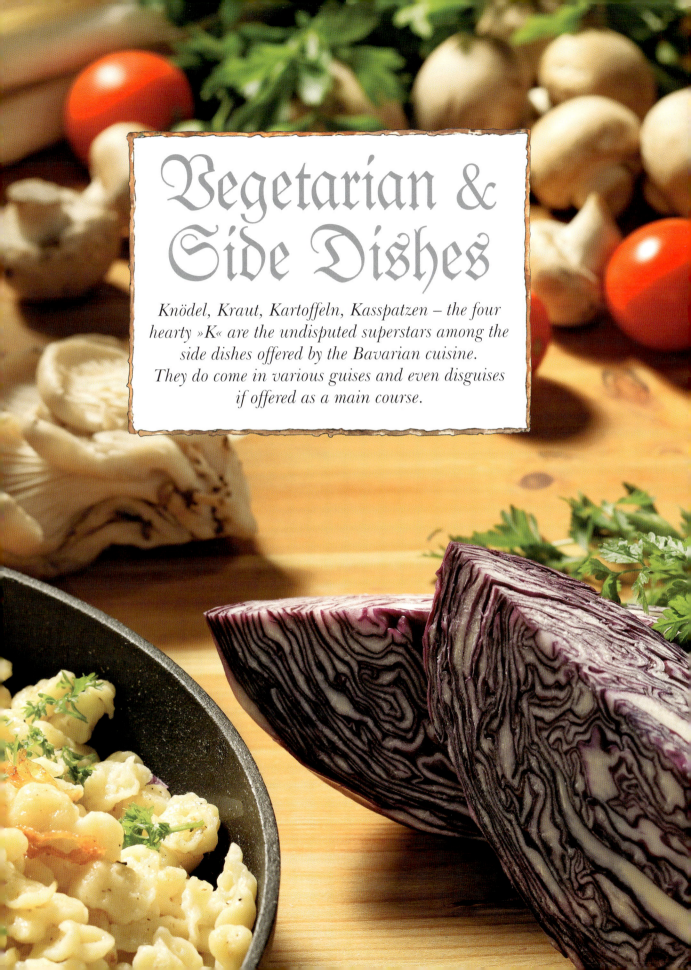

Vegetarian & Side Dishes

Knödel, Kraut, Kartoffeln, Kasspatzen – the four hearty »K« are the undisputed superstars among the side dishes offered by the Bavarian cuisine. They do come in various guises and even disguises if offered as a main course.

Vegetarian

Allgäuer Kasspatzen
Spaetzle with Emmental Cheese and Fried Onion Rings

Serves 4

3 1/2 cups all-purpose flour
1 teaspoon salt
6 eggs
2 cups Emmental cheese
5 onions
6 tablespoons butter
freshly ground pepper
freshly ground nutmeg

1 Sift the flour into a bowl. Add the salt and whisk in 1 1/2 cups of water. Add the eggs and whisk until fluffy. Cover with a kitchen towel and allow to rest.

2 Grate the cheese coarsely. Peel the onions and cut into fine rings. Melt the butter in a pan and fry the onions until golden.

3 Bring 3 quarts of salted water to the boil in a large saucepan. Press the dough through the spaetzle maker into the boiling water. Leave to boil for 3 minutes until the spaetzle rise to the surface. Repeat until the dough has been used up.

4 Immediately remove the speatzle with a slotted ladle, drain well and put into an oven-proof dish. Sprinkle some cheese over each layer of spaetzle and season with pepper and nutmeg.

5 Keep the spaetzle warm in a preheated oven. Serve on warm plates garnished with roasted onions.

Our chef suggests:

*3 1/2 cups of flour suffice if the spaetzle are to be served as a side dish.
For a main course, you will need 5 cups flour, 1 teaspoon of salt,
3 1/2 cups water, 8 eggs and 3 cups cheese.
In the old days, the dough was made with milk instead of water
to reduce the number of eggs required. Spaetzle are best served with
a green salad or a mixed salad.*

Vegetarian

Überbackene Pfannkuchen
Asparagus Crepes au Gratin

Serves 4

For the crepes:
2/3 cup milk
2/3 cup dry white wine
3 eggs, 2½ cups all-purpose flour
1 teaspoon grated lemon rind
salt
freshly ground nutmeg
2 tablespoons chopped parsley
6 tablespoons butter

For the filling:
2 pounds white asparagus
salt, sugar
1 teaspoon butter

For the gratin:
4 tomatoes, 1 onion
2 tablespoons butter
2 ounces crème fraîche
½ cup Emmental cheese

1 Whisk the milk, the white wine and the eggs in a bowl. Add the flour, the lemon rind, salt, 1 pinch of nutmeg, the chopped parsley and whisk well. Allow to rest for 30 minutes.

2 Peel and trim the asparagus, then tie the asparagus together with kitchen thread.

3 Bring 3 quarts of water to the boil in a large saucepan. Add salt, 1 pinch of sugar and 1 teaspoon of butter. Boil the asparagus for 10 to 15 minutes until soft. Remove the asparagus and drain on kitchen paper. Heat the oven to 450 °F.

4 Bake 12 thin crepes in a buttered non-stick griddle. Place 2 to 4 asparagus on each crepe and roll. Grease an oven-proof dish and place the asparagus crepes inside.

5 To peel the tomatoes, make an X with a sharp knife on the bottom, dip them into boiling water for 1 minute, remove the tomatoes and set aside to cool. Peel, de-seed and dice finely. Peel the onion and dice finely.

6 Melt the butter in a pan and fry the tomato and the onion briefly. Add the crème fraîche. Pour the gratin-mix over the crepes.

7 Grate the cheese and sprinkle over the crepes. Bake the crepes in the preheated oven on the middle rung until the cheese has melted.

Vegetarian

Gemischte Schwammerl
Mushrooms in Cream Sauce with Bread Dumplings

Serves 4

For the dumplings:
10 stale hard bread rolls
salt
2 cups milk
½ onion
1 bunch parsley
1 bunch chives
1 tablespoon butter
3 eggs

For the mushrooms:
3 cups white mushrooms
1 ½ cups brown mushrooms
1 ½ cups oyster mushrooms
1 onion
1 clove garlic
3 tablespoons butter
salt
freshly ground pepper
freshly ground nutmeg
2 tablespoons all-purpose flour
¾ cup dry white wine
½ quart cream

1 Cut the stale bread rolls (they should be hard and dry) into thin slices. Add them to a bowl and season with salt. Pour the lukewarm milk over the bread. Cover and allow to rest for 20 minutes. Peel the onion and dice finely. Wash the parsley and the chives and shake dry. Pluck the leaves and chop finely. Cut the chives into fine rolls.

2 Melt the butter in a pan and fry the onions until golden. Add the onions, the eggs and half of the parsley to the bread-mix and knead well. Moisten your hands and shape 8 dumplings.

3 Bring 3 quarts of salted water to the boil in a large saucepan. Add the dumplings and allow to simmer for 15 minutes. Make sure the water does not boil! Remove the dumplings with a slotted ladle and drain.

4 Trim and rub the mushrooms clean and cut into quarters. Peel the onion and the garlic and dice finely. Melt 1 tablespoon of butter in a pan and fry the onion and the garlic until transparent. Add the mushrooms and fry for 10 minutes over low heat. Season with salt, pepper and 1 pinch of nutmeg.

5 Melt the remaining butter in a small saucepan, add the flour and fry until golden. Pour in the white wine and the cream and bring to the boil once. Add the mushrooms to the sauce. Sprinkle with the remaining parsley and half of the chives and season with salt and pepper.

6 Serve the mushrooms on warm plates. Place two dumplings in the middle and sprinkle with the remaining chives.

Röstkartoffeln
Fried Potatoes with Onions

Serves 4
1 pound waxy potatoes
salt
1 onion
3 tablespoons butter
freshly ground pepper
½ bunch chives

1 Wash the potatoes and boil them in salted water for 20 minutes. Rinse under cold water, then peel. Allow to cool briefly.

2 Cut the potatoes into even slices. Peel the onion, cut into half. Then cut into fine half-moon shapes.

3 Melt the butter in a non-stick pan and fry the potatoes until golden-brown. Then add the onions and season with salt and pepper.

4 Wash the chives, shake dry and cut into fine rolls. Place the fried potatoes on a plate and sprinkle with chives.

Our chef suggests:

*If you like, you can season the fried potatoes
with 1 pinch of cumin.
Leftover boiled potatoes can also be used.
If you want to save on butter,
cover the pan while frying.*

Vegetarian

Kartoffelschmarrn
Shredded Potatoes with Sour Cream

Serves 4

5 medium-sized mealy potatoes

salt

1 cup all-purpose flour

clarified butter, for frying

3 tablespoons sour cream

1 Wash the potatoes and boil them in salted water for 20 to 25 minutes. Drain and allow to cool briefly.

2 Peel the potatoes and, while still warm, press them through the potato press into a shallow bowl.

3 Allow the potatoes to cool completely. Add salt and flour. Knead until the dough turns crumbly.

4 Melt the clarified butter in a griddle and fry the potato-mix until golden-brown, turning it over several times.

5 Add the sour cream and allow the shredded potatoes to marinate briefly.

Our chef suggests:

*Leftover boiled potatoes can be used for this dish, too.
Peel the potatoes and grate them. If you want to save on butter,
prepare the dish in the oven.
Heat some oil in an oven-proof dish and bake the
potato-flour-mix until golden-brown, turning it over several times.
As a side dish, shredded potatoes go well with hearty sauces,
cabbage or sauerkraut. You might also like to try it
with apple mousse or cranberry sauce.*

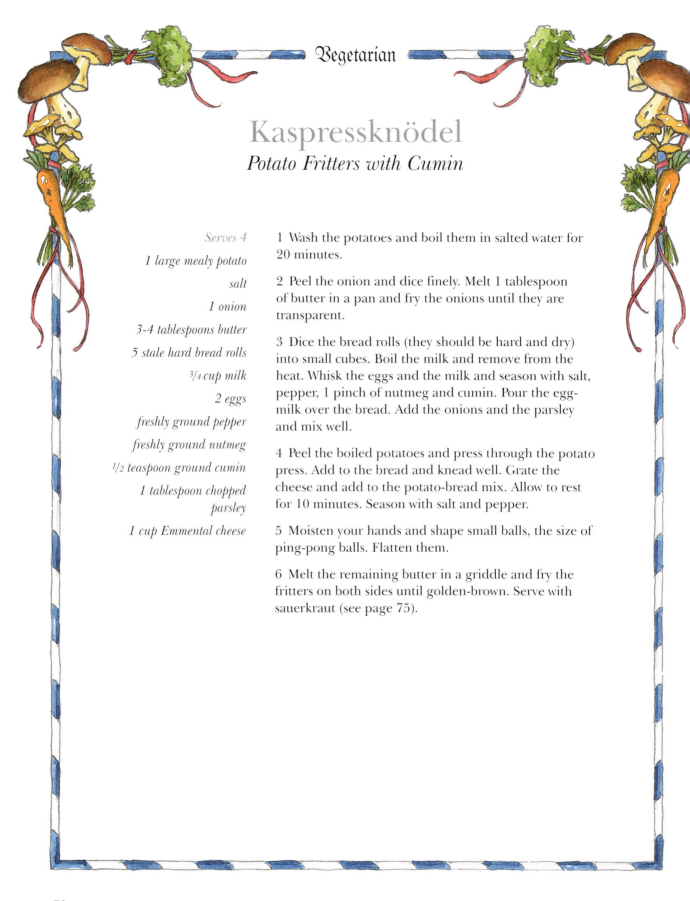

Vegetarian

Kaspressknödel
Potato Fritters with Cumin

Serves 4

1 large mealy potato
salt
1 onion
3-4 tablespoons butter
5 stale hard bread rolls
¾ cup milk
2 eggs
freshly ground pepper
freshly ground nutmeg
½ teaspoon ground cumin
1 tablespoon chopped parsley
1 cup Emmental cheese

1 Wash the potatoes and boil them in salted water for 20 minutes.

2 Peel the onion and dice finely. Melt 1 tablespoon of butter in a pan and fry the onions until they are transparent.

3 Dice the bread rolls (they should be hard and dry) into small cubes. Boil the milk and remove from the heat. Whisk the eggs and the milk and season with salt, pepper, 1 pinch of nutmeg and cumin. Pour the egg-milk over the bread. Add the onions and the parsley and mix well.

4 Peel the boiled potatoes and press through the potato press. Add to the bread and knead well. Grate the cheese and add to the potato-bread mix. Allow to rest for 10 minutes. Season with salt and pepper.

5 Moisten your hands and shape small balls, the size of ping-pong balls. Flatten them.

6 Melt the remaining butter in a griddle and fry the fritters on both sides until golden-brown. Serve with sauerkraut (see page 75).

Reiberknödel
Original Munich Potato Dumplings with Nutmeg

Serves 4
2 pounds mealy potatoes
salt
1 egg
2 heaping tablespoons cornflour
freshly ground pepper
freshly ground nutmeg

1 Wash half of the potatoes and boil them in salted water for 20 minutes. Rinse them under cold water and peel. Press through a potato press into a shallow bowl.

2 Wash and peel the remaining potatoes and grate them finely. Put them into a kitchen towel and squeeze out any liquid.

3 Mix the boiled and uncooked potatoes with the egg and the cornstarch. Season with salt, pepper and plenty of nutmeg.

4 Moisten your hands and shape dumplings. Bring 3 quarts of salted water to the boil in a large saucepan and allow the dumplings to simmer for 15 to 20 minutes until they are done. Remove the dumplings with a slotted ladle, drain and serve immediately.

Our chef suggests:

Potato dumplings can also be prepared with uncooked potatoes only. Grate the potatoes and squeeze them dry. In 3 cups of hot milk allow 3 tablespoons of grits to swell. Add to the potatoes. Season with salt. With moist hands shape dumplings. You can also place fried bread cubes into the middle of each dumpling. Dumplings go very well with roast pork or pork knuckles, Boeuf à la mode and roast goose.

Vegetarian

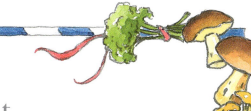

Sauerkraut
The Genuine Sauerkraut with Five Spices

Serves 4

2 onions

¼ cup clarified butter

1 pound uncooked sauerkraut

¾ cup dry white wine

¾ cup beef consommé (see page 52)

salt, sugar

1 bay leaf, allspice, peppercorns, cloves, cumin

1 mealy potato

1 Peel the onions and cut into half. Then cut into fine half-moon shapes. Melt the clarified butter in a pan and fry the onions until they are transparent.

2 Rinse the sauerkraut under running water, drain and add to the pan. Pour over the wine and the beef consommé. Season with salt and 1 pinch of sugar.

3 Put the bay leaf, the allspice, the peppercorns and cloves as well as the cumin into an empty (unused!) teabag. Tie it up and add to the sauerkraut.

4 Wash and peel the potato, grate finely and add to the sauerkraut.

5 Cover the sauerkraut and allow to simmer for 40 to 50 minutes. Remove the teabag before serving.

Vegetarian

Schupfnudeln
Finger Noodles with Sauerkraut

Serves 4

¾ pound (2 large) mealy potatoes

salt

1 ½ cups all-purpose flour

2 tablespoons butter

1 egg yolk

freshly ground pepper

freshly ground nutmeg

3 ounces clarified butter

1 Wash and boil the potatoes in salted water for 20 minutes. Rinse under cold water, peel and press through the potato press into a bowl. Add flour, butter, egg yolk, salt, pepper and nutmeg and knead into a dough.

2 Flour the work surface and roll out the potato dough into a 1 inch thick rope. Cut off 2 inch long noodle fingers.

3 Bring 3 quarts of salted water to the boil in a large saucepan. Allow the noodles to simmer briefly. Remove the noodles with a slotted ladle and drain.

4 Melt the clarified butter in a griddle and fry the well-drained noodles until golden-brown, turning them over several times. Serve with sauerkraut (see page 75).

Our chef suggests:

Finger noodles make a very nice side dish to accompany Bavarian stews. If served as a main course, they can be mixed with sauerkraut and fried. Pour over some melted butter and sprinkle with fried onions and chopped chives before serving.

Vegetarian

Blaukraut
Red Cabbage with Apples

Serves 4
2 pounds red cabbage
2 onions
2 apples
¼ cup clarified butter
1 tablespoon sugar
1 bay leaf, allspice, peppercorns
cloves
1 cinnamon stick
4 tablespoons red wine vinegar, salt
½ cup red wine
½ cup beef consommé (see page 52)
3 tablespoons red current jelly

1 Remove the discolored leaves from the cabbage, quarter and cut out the stalk. Cut the quarters into fine strips. Alternatively, you can shred the cabbage finely on a grater. Wash and drain in a colander. Peel the onions and cut into fine strips. Peel the apples, quarter, core and cut into fine slices.

2 Melt the clarified butter in a pan, add the sugar and allow to caramelize. Add the onions and the apples and fry until soft. Put the bay leaf, the allspice, the peppercorns and cloves as well as the cinnamon stick into an unused teabag and tie it up.

3 Add the cabbage to the onion and apples and fry briefly. Add the herbs in the teabag and pour over the vinegar to preserve the color of the cabbage. Season with salt and pepper. Pour over the red wine and the beef consommé.

4 Cover and allow to simmer for 50 to 60 minutes. Add some more wine if necessary.

5 Before serving remove the teabag and mix under the red current jelly. Season with salt and pepper.

Vegetarian

Bayerisch Kraut
Bavarian Cabbage Salad with Bacon

Serves 4

2 pounds cabbage

2 onions

4 ounces bacon

2 1/2 tablespoons clarified butter

1 tablespoon sugar

2 tablespoons white wine vinegar

salt

freshly ground pepper

2 teaspoons cumin

1/2 cup beef consommé (see page 52)

1 Remove the discolored leaves from the cabbage, quarter and cut out the stalk. Shred the cabbage finely on a grater. Wash and drain in a colander.

2 Peel the onions and dice finely. Dice the bacon into small cubes.

3 Melt the clarified butter in a pan, add the sugar and allow to caramelize. Add the bacon and the onions and fry until soft. Pour over the vinegar and season with salt, pepper and cumin.

4 Add the beef consommé, cover and allow to simmer for 50 minutes over low heat. Season with salt and pepper before serving.

Our chef suggests:

If you do not care for bacon, you need not add it. You can also prepare the cabbage in a pressure cooker. That reduces the cooking time to 10 minutes.

Fish

Whether fried, baked or smoked – all that splashes about in Bavaria's many rivers and lakes, be it perch, trout or pikeperch, tastes best with a glass of fresh beer. After all, »fish need to swim«.

Fish

Gedünstetes Rotbarschfilet
Rosefish with Vegetable Juliennes and White Wine Sauce

Serves 4

1 onion
2 carrots
½ pound celeriac
1 small leek
½ cup butter
salt
freshly ground pepper
4 rosefish fillets
2 tablespoons lemon juice
3 tablespoons all-purpose flour
½ cup dry white wine
½ cup good fish stock
½ cup cream
1 egg yolk

1 Peel the onion and dice finely. Set aside. Peel the carrot and the celeriac, trim and wash the leek. Cut the carrot, celeriac and leek into thin strips.

2 Melt half of the butter in a pan, add the vegetable strips and fry over low heat until soft, stirring frequently. If necessary add some water. Season with salt and pepper.

3 Rinse the fish fillets under running water and dab dry. Sprinkle with lemon juice and season with salt and pepper. Mix 3 tablespoons of butter and 3 tablespoons of four and knead into a small ball.

4 Melt the remaining butter in a pan and fry the onions until transparent. Pour over the white wine and the fish stock. Add the fish fillets and allow to poach for 10 minutes over low heat.

5 Remove the fish fillets from the pan, place on warm plates and keep warm. Add the flour-butter ball to the sauce and bring to the boil briefly. Then strain through a fine colander and return to the pan. Whisk the cream and the egg yolk and add to the sauce. Season with salt and pepper.

6 Pour the sauce over the fish and garnish with the vegetables. Serve with boiled rice.

Fish

Forelle »blau«
Trout au Bleu

Serves 4
For the stock:

1 onion, 1 carrot

¼ pound celeriac

1 small leek
(only the white trunk)

2 sprigs of parsley

1 sprig of tarragon

5 peppercorns

2 tablespoons salt, 1 tablespoon sugar

1 bay leaf

¾ cup vinegar

¾ cup white wine

For the trout:

4 fresh trout (cleaned but not scaled!)

4 tablespoons vinegar

1 Peel the onion, the carrot and the celeriac. Trim and wash the leek. Cut the vegetables into fine strips. Wash the herbs and shake dry. Grind the peppercorns with a mortar.

2 Bring 2 quarts of water to the boil in a large fish pot, add the vegetables, the herbs and spices, the vinegar and the wine and bring to the boil. Reduce the heat, cover and allow to simmer for 35 minutes.

3 Wash the trout carefully, place on a platter and sprinkle with vinegar to preserve their blue color.

4 Put the trout into the hot stock (they should be totally submerged) and bring to the boil. Skim the scum. When boiling, immediately remove the pot from the heat. Allow the trout to marinate for 10 minutes until tender. The fish are ready to eat when the eyes turn white and the back fin can be pulled out easily.

5 Place the trout on warm plates and garnish with lemon slices and parsley. Serve immediately with boiled potatoes (see page 84) and a green salad.

Our chef suggests:

When cooking fish, three rules apply:
1. clean: Whole fish are scaled, gutted and washed.
Fish fillets are only washed.
2. marinate: Fish and fish fillets are sprinkled with vinegar or lemon juice. The acid renders the meat firmer and improves the taste.
3. salt: Fish is only salted just before cooking.
Otherwise, the fish becomes dry.

Fish

Forelle »Müllerin Art«
Trout »Müllerin Art«

Serves 4

1 ½ pounds waxy potatoes
salt
4 trout (cleaned and scaled)
1 lemon
freshly ground white pepper
6 tablespoons all-purpose flour
6 tablespoons clarified butter
½ bunch parsley
5 tablespoons butter

1 Peel and wash the potatoes, then cut in half lengthwise. Put the potatoes into a pot with cold salted water and bring to the boil. Cover and cook for 20 to 25 minutes until soft. Drain, allow the steam to evaporate, cover and keep warm.

2 Wash the trout and dab dry. Wash the lemon, rub dry, cut in half and squeeze one half. Sprinkle the lemon juice over the outside and the inside of the trout. Season with salt and pepper.

3 Spread the flour on a plate, roll the trout in the flour and coat well.

4 Melt the clarified butter in two large frying pans. Fry the trout over high heat briefly, then continue to fry over low heat for 8 minutes until golden-brown. Turn the trout over and fry the other side until golden-brown.

5 Cut the remaining lemon half into thin slices. Wash the parsley and shake dry. Pluck the leaves and chop finely.

6 Place the trout on warm plates, garnish with lemon slices and sprinkle with parsley. Melt the butter in a pan and pour over the trout.

Our chef suggests:

Potatoes that have been boiled in their skin can also be served with trout Müllerin Art. And don't forget the green salad!

Fish

Wirsingpflanzerl
Savoy Cabbage Fritters with Salmon Sauce

Serves 4
For the fritters:
2 stale hard bread rolls
1 3/4 pounds Savoy cabbage
salt
2 eggs
freshly ground pepper
3 tablespoons oil

For the salmon sauce:
1 small onion
1 tablespoon oil
1 1/2 cup sour cream
2 tablespoons cream cheese
2 drops Tabasco
salt, freshly ground pepper
sugar
1 teaspoon cornstarch
7 ounces smoked salmon
1/2 bunch dill

1 Add the stale bread rolls (they must be hard and dry) to a bowl and pour over 2 cups of lukewarm water. Allow to soak. Bring 3 quarts of salted water to the boil in a large saucepan.

2 Remove the discolored leaves from the cabbage, quarter and cut out the stalk.

3 Cook the cabbage in the salted water for 10 minutes, drain and allow to cool.

4 Chop the cabbage finely with a large knife or a mincing knife. With your hands squeeze the bread rolls dry. Add the cabbage and the eggs and knead well. Season with salt and pepper.

5 Moisten your hands and shape flat fritters. Heat the oil in a griddle and fry the fritters for 15 minutes on each side over low heat until they are golden-brown. Keep warm.

6 Peel the onion and dice finely. Heat the oil in a pan and fry the onions until transparent. Pour over 1 cup of water and mix in the sour cream and the cream cheese. Season with Tabasco, salt, pepper and 1 pinch of sugar. Dissolve the cornstarch in 1 tablespoon of cold water and add to the sauce to thicken.

7 Cut the salmon into fine strips. Wash the dill, shake dry and pluck the tips. Mix the dill and the salmon under the sauce just before serving.

8 Place the fritters on a plate, add the salmon sauce and serve with either boiled rice or potatoes.

Fish

Seezungenrouladen
Sole Roulades with Swiss Chard and Tomato Sauce

Serves 4
For the roulades:
8 large Swiss chard leaves
salt
100 g fresh wild mushrooms
4 tablespoons butter
freshly ground pepper
4 unpeeled shrimps
8 sole fillets
8 stalks of chives

For the tomato sauce:
1 shallot
2 cups tomato puree
1 1/4 cup brandy
4 tablespoons cream
salt, freshly ground pepper
sugar

1 Wash the Swiss chard leaves and cut out center ribs. Bring 3 quarts of salted water to the boil in a large saucepan and cook the leaves until soft. Drain and rinse under cold water. Spread the leaves on kitchen paper.

2 Trim the mushrooms, rub clean and cut into fine slices. Melt 2 tablespoons of butter in a pan and fry the mushrooms until soft. Season with salt and pepper.

3 Wash the shrimps, add to a bowl and pour over boiling water. Drain and pull off the heads. Peel the tails and de-vein. Reserve the heads and the tails.

4 Wash the sole fillets and dab dry. Take 2 leaves and place 2 fillets, 1 shrimp and some mushrooms on top. Roll up and fasten with chives. Repeat until ingredients are used up. Keep the 4 roulades refrigerated.

5 Peel the shallot and dice finely. Melt the remaining butter and fry the shallot until transparent. Add the reserved shrimp heads and tails and fry while stirring. Pour over the brandy and allow to simmer for a few minutes. Add the tomato puree and cook for another 5 minutes. Mix under the cream and bring just to the boil. Remove the sauce from the heat, strain through a fine colander and season with salt, pepper and 1 pinch of sugar.

6 Place the sole roulades on a steaming rack and steam them over boiling salted water for 20 minutes. Place the sole roulades on warm plates and serve with tagliatelle, rice or potatoes.

Fish

Fischpflanzerl
Fish Fritters with Breadcrumb Crust

Serves 4

1 pound white meat fish fillets (e.g. cod, sole, rosefish)
1 tablespoon lemon juice
1 stale hard bread roll
1 cup lukewarm milk
½ bunch parsley
½ bunch marjoram
1 onion
1 egg
4 ounces sausage meat
salt
freshly ground pepper
paprika
8 tablespoons breadcrumbs
oil, for frying

1 Wash the fish fillets and dab dry. Dice the fish into small cubes, add to a bowl and sprinkle with lemon juice. Set aside.

2 Add the bread roll (it must be hard and dry) to a small bowl, pour over the lukewarm milk and allow to soak.

3 Wash the herbs and shake dry. Pluck the leaves and chop finely. Peel the onion and dice finely.

4 With your hands squeeze the bread roll dry. Put the bread and the fish through a grinder.

5 Add the egg, the ground meat, the herbs and the onion to the fish mix. Season with salt, pepper, and 1 pinch of paprika and knead well.

6 Moisten your hands and shape flat fritters. Spread the breadcrumbs on a plate. Coat the fritters with breadcrumbs.

7 Heat the oil in a pan or in a deep fryer to 350 °F and fry the fritters until golden. Serve with potato salad, or boiled potatoes sprinkled with parsley and green salad.

Fish

Gebratener Zander
Pikeperch with Sauce Hollandaise

Serves 4

For the fish:

4 pikeperch fillets (boned but not skinned)

juice of ½ lemon

4 tablespoons butter

salt

freshly ground pepper

For the sauce hollandaise:

2 shallots

1 teaspoon white peppercorns

1 ¼ cup dry white wine

1 cup white wine vinegar

3 egg yolks

½ pound warm melted butter

cayenne pepper, sugar

½ bunch parsley

1 Wash the pikeperch fillets and dab dry. Sprinkle with lemon juice.

2 Melt the butter in a pan and fry the fillets for 5 minutes, skin down, over low heat. Remove the pan from the heat, turn the fillets over and allow to rest until the meat turns white. Drain on kitchen paper and season with salt and pepper.

3 Peel the shallots and dice finely. Grind the peppercorns with a mortar. Add the shallots, the peppercorns, the white wine, the vinegar and 1 cup of water to a small saucepan and bring to the boil. Continue to cook until the sauce is reduced by two thirds. Strain the sauce through a fine colander into a small metal bowl.

4 Place the bowl over a pan of hot water, add the egg yolks and whisk until frothy. Whisk in the melted butter until the sauce is smooth. Season with salt, 1 pinch of cayenne pepper and 1 pinch of sugar.

5 Wash the parsley and shake dry. Pluck the leaves and chop finely. Place the fish fillets on warm plates and sprinkle with parsley. Serve with Sauce Hollandaise and boiled potatoes sprinkled with parsley.

Meat

Well-tried and world-famous. Roast pork, roast pork knuckles and Böfflamott will satisfy even the mightiest of appetites. And if you have these authentic Bavarian dishes with a glass of beer, you will soon find yourself in gourmet heaven.

Meat

Wiesnhendl
Roast Chicken with Potato Salad

Serves 4

2 chickens
(2 ½ pounds each)
¾ cup oil
salt
freshly ground pepper
paprika
curry powder
dried thyme
freshly ground nutmeg
4 sprigs of parsley

1 Wash the chickens, also on the inside, and dab dry. Mix the oil, salt and pepper, 1 teaspoon of paprika, 1 teaspoon of curry powder, thyme and ½ teaspoon of nutmeg into a paste.

2 Coat the chickens with the paste, inside and out. Wash the parsley and shake dry. Place two sprigs of parsley inside each chicken. Heat the oven to 325 °F.

3 First, roast the chickens, breast side down. When they turn golden-brown, turn them over. In total, roast the chickens for 60 to 90 minutes in a preheated oven, basting frequently.

4 Remove the chickens from the oven and cut into half. Place the chicken halves on plates and serve with potato salad (see page 62), green salad or bread.

Our chef suggests:

*If fresh chicken are unavailable, use frozen chicken.
Thaw them in the refrigerator one day before cooking.
Remove the giblets and any fat. Wash well under running
cold water and dab dry.*

Hähnchenbrustfilet
Browned Chicken Breasts on Tomato Noodles

Serves 4

For the chicken breasts:

4 chicken breasts, 3 eggs

2 tablespoons grated Parmesan cheese

1 cup all-purpose flour

salt, freshly ground pepper

4 tablespoons butter

For the tomato noodles:

1/2 pound mixed vegetables (for instance: 1 carrot, 1 onion, 1/2 celeriac)

4 ounces bacon

5 tablespoons butter

2 tablespoons all-purpose flour

2 1/2 cups tomato paste

1 1/2 cups red wine

2 cups good vegetable stock

2 cloves garlic

1 bay leaf

1 teaspoon each dried thyme, rosemary, sage, oregano, juniper berries

4 tomatoes

salt, freshly ground pepper

sugar, 1 pound tagliatelle

1 Wash the chicken breasts and dab dry. Whisk the eggs, the parmesan and 1 tablespoon of flour to make a batter. Season the meat with salt and pepper. Dip the breasts in the batter and roll in the remaining flour.

2 Melt the butter in a griddle and fry the chicken breasts for 5 minutes on each side until golden-brown.

3 Peel the vegetables and dice finely. Dice the bacon into small cubes. Melt the butter in a pan and fry the vegetables and the bacon.

4 Sprinkle with 2 tablespoons of flour and mix in the tomato paste. Pour over the red wine and the vegetable stock and bring to the boil, stirring constantly. Peel the garlic and soften it with a blade.

5 Add the garlic, the herbs and the spices to the tomato sauce and allow to simmer for 30 minutes. To peel the tomatoes, make an X with a sharp knife on the bottom, dip them into boiling water for 1 minute, remove the tomatoes and set aside to cool. Peel, de-seed and dice. Set aside.

6 Strain the sauce through a fine colander and season with salt, pepper and 1 pinch of sugar. Add the diced tomatoes and bring the sauce to the boil.

7 Cook the noodles in plenty of salted water according to package instructions. Drain and mix with the tomato sauce.

8 Remove the chicken breasts from the griddle, dab dry and make a shallow diagonal cut. Place the tomato noodles on warm plates and serve with the chicken breasts on top.

Gebratene Ente
Roast Duck à l'Orange

Serves 4

For the duck:

1 duck (4-4 1/2 pounds)

salt

freshly ground pepper

1 1/4 cups good chicken consommé

4 tablespoons oil

For the sauce:

1 onion

2 ounces celeriac

2 ounces leek (only the white trunk)

2 tablespoons butter

1 1/2 cups demi-glace (see page 121)

2 tablespoons sugar

1/2 cup ruby Port

1/2 cup fresh orange juice

2 tablespoons balsamico vinegar

1 Heat the oven to 420 °F. Wash the duck, also on the inside, and dab dry. Season with salt and pepper.

2 Heat the chicken consommé in a small pan. Heat the oil in a roasting tin and place the duck inside, breast side down. Add the hot consommé and roast the duck for 30 minutes on the middle rung in the oven. Then reduce the temperature to 350 °F.

3 Continue roasting the duck for 90 minutes, basting occasionally. When the duck turns golden-brown, turn it over.

4 For the sauce, peel the onion and the celeriac, trim and wash the leek. Dice the vegetables finely.

5 Remove the duck from the roasting tin. Carve the duck into portions and keep warm. Reserve the carcass.

6 Skim the fat from the roasting juices. Melt the butter in a pan and fry the vegetables, stirring constantly. Add the carcass, the roasting juices and the demi-glace. Bring the sauce to the boil and cook for 5 minutes. Strain through a fine colander and keep warm.

7 Caramelize the sugar in a small pan, add the Port, the orange juice, the balsamico vinegar and the duck sauce and cook for 3 minutes. Season with salt and pepper.

8 Arrange the duck on plates, pour over the sauce and serve with potato dumplings and red cabbage or salad.

Meat

Gänseklein
Goose Giblets in White Wine Sauce

Serves 4

1 onion

2 cloves garlic

1 bunch soupgreens (1 carrot, 1 piece of celeriac, 1 small leek and 1 sprig of parsley)

1 pound giblets and wings

3 tablespoons goose dripping

salt

freshly ground pepper

3 tablespoons all-purpose flour

¾ cup dry white wine

3 ½ cups good chicken consommé

1 lemon

1 bouquet garni (a few sprigs each of thyme, rosemary and marjoram)

1 bay leaf

sugar

1 Peel the onion and the garlic and chop finely. Wash, trim and peel the soupgreens and dice finely.

2 Wash the goose meat and dab dry. Melt the dripping in a pan and fry the meat until golden-brown. Season with salt and pepper. Remove the meat from the pan and set aside.

3 In the same pan fry the onion, garlic and the diced soupgreen. Sprinkle with flour and pour over the white wine and the consommé.

4 Wash the lemon and rub dry. Grate the rind finely. Wash the bouquet garni and shake dry. Add the grated lemon rind, the herbs, the bay leaf and the meat to the sauce and cook for one hour until the meat is tender.

5 Remove the meat and vegetables from the sauce. Strain the sauce through a fine colander and season with salt, pepper and 1 pinch of sugar. Pluck the meat off the bones and return to the sauce.

6 Serve this dish with bread dumplings and a salad or with boiled potatoes (see page 84).

Meat

Putengeschnetzeltes
Turkey Ragout with Mushrooms

Serves 4

1 1/4 pounds turkey meat

1 1/4 pounds white mushrooms

1 tablespoon oil

salt

freshly ground pepper

1/2 teaspoon paprika

1/4 cup dry white wine

3/4 cup cream

1 Wash the turkey meat and dab dry. Cut into bite-size strips.

2 Rub the mushrooms clean and cut into thin slices.

3 Heat the oil in a pan and fry the meat until golden-brown. Season with salt and pepper. Add the mushrooms and fry briefly.

4 Pour over the white wine and reduce by half.

5 Add the cream, season with salt and pepper, and bring to the boil once.

6 Place the ragout on warm plates and serve with boiled rice or spaetzle.

Our chef suggests:

The sauce becomes extra delicious if you add 4 tablespoons of finely chopped herbs, for example parsley, chives or chervil.

Meat

Schweinshaxe
Pork Knuckle with Potato Dumpling and Cabbage Salad

Serves 4

4 legs of pork with bones (1 pound each)

salt

freshly ground pepper

1 sprig of rosemary

½ cup oil

2 onions

1 clove garlic

1 large carrot

3 ounces celeriac

3 ounces streaky smoked bacon

3 ½ cups lager beer

2 cups beef consommé (see page 52)

2 tablespoons butter

2 tablespoons all-purpose flour

1 Heat the oven to 450 °F. Wash the pork knuckles, dab dry and season with salt and pepper. Wash the rosemary and shake dry.

2 Place the knuckles next to each other inside a roasting tin, sprinkle with oil and add the rosemary. Roast the knuckles on the bottom rung in the oven for 30 minutes.

3 Meanwhile peel the onions, the garlic, the carrot and the celeriac and dice finely. Dice the bacon into small cubes. When the knuckles have been in the oven for 30 minutes, add the diced vegetables and reduce the heat to 350 °F. Continue to roast for 45 minutes.

4 Add the beer and the consommé to the roasting juices and continue roasting for 60 to 90 minutes.

5 Remove the knuckles from the roasting tin, place them on a baking tray and return them to the oven with the heat turned off. Skim the fat from the roasting juices and blend the sauce until smooth. Strain the sauce through a fine colander and bring to the boil.

6 Mix the butter and the flour and knead into a small ball. Whisk into the sauce in morsels to thicken.

7 Season the sauce with salt and pepper. Place the knuckles on warm plates. Serve with potato dumplings (see page 74) and cabbage salad with bacon (see page 61).

Meat

Saure Schweinenierchen
Pork Kidneys with Gherkins

Serves 4

1 pound pork kidneys
2 onions
3 gherkins
4 tablespoons clarified butter
2 tablespoons red wine
1 tablespoon lemon juice
1 ½ cups demi-glace
(see page 121)
salt
freshly ground pepper

1 Wash the kidneys and peel off the membrane. Cut into half lengthwise. Remove the hard core. Wash again and soak in cold water. Set aside.

2 Peel the onions and dice finely. Cut the gherkins into fine strips.

3 Remove the kidneys from the water and dab dry. Cut into fine slices.

4 Melt 2 tablespoons of clarified butter in a pan and fry the kidneys until brown. Remove the kidneys from the pan. Set aside and keep warm.

5 Melt the remaining butter in the pan and fry the onions until transparent. Pour over the vinegar and lemon juice and reduce by half. Add the demi-glace and simmer. Do not let it bubble.

6 Season the kidneys with salt and pepper and add to the sauce together with the gherkins. Season the sauce with salt and pepper. Serve with fried potatoes and a salad.

Our chef suggests:

*Kidneys should not be cooked too long
or they turn leathery.
That is why they should be seasoned
only before serving.*

Meat

Braumeistersteak
Brewmaster's Pork Steak with Baked Potatoes

Serves 4

For the steaks:

1 tablespoon soy sauce

2 drops Tabasco

1 teaspoon steak seasoning

½ teaspoon dried basil

½ teaspoon dried oregano

6 tablespoons oil

4 pork steaks (from the neck; 4 ½ ounces each)

Also:

1 bunch mixed herbs (e.g. parsley, chervil, tarragon, dill)

½ cup soft butter

1 teaspoon lemon juice

Worcester Sauce, salt

freshly ground pepper

4 large baking potatoes

1 bunch chives

1 cup crème fraîche or thick sour cream

1 For the marinade, mix the soy sauce, the Tabasco, the steak seasoning, the dried herbs and 4 tablespoons of oil. Wash the steaks and dab dry. Coat the steaks on both sides with the marinade. Place the steaks in a bowl, pour over the remaining marinade and allow to stand for 24 to 48 hours, turning the steaks over once.

2 For the herb butter, wash the herbs, shake dry, pluck the leaves and chop finely. Whisk the butter in a bowl. Add the herbs, the lemon juice and 1 dash of Worcester Sauce and season with salt and pepper. Place the butter on a piece of metal foil and shape into a ball. Keep refrigerated.

3 Heat the oven to 395 °F. Wash the potatoes and wrap them up in metal foil (shiny side next to the potato skin). Place the potatoes on the top rung in the oven and bake for 60 to 90 minutes until soft. Wash the chives, shake dry and cut into fine rolls. Add to the crème fraiche and season with salt and pepper. Keep refrigerated.

4 Heat the oil in a pan. Remove the steaks from the marinade, drain slightly, and fry them for 7 minutes on each side until brown.

5 Remove the metal foil from the herb butter and cut the herb butter into slices. Remove the metal foil from the baked potatoes and cut a cross in the top of each potato.

6 Place the steaks on warm plates and put the herb butter on top. Serve with the baked potatoes and a dollop of crème fraîche.

Schweinebraten
Roast Pork with Dark Beer Sauce

Serves 4

2 1/2 pounds boneless pork shoulder (with skin)

salt

freshly ground pepper

1 teaspoon dried marjoram

1 onion

1 clove garlic

1 bunch soupgreen (see page 98)

1 tomato

2 ounces crust of a slice of rye bread

1 1/4 cups dark beer

1 Heat the oven to 385 °F. Wash the meat and dab dry. Season the meat with salt, pepper and marjoram and place inside a roasting tin.

2 Pour over 1 cup of hot water and roast the meat on the medium rung of the oven for 30 minutes.

3 Peel the onion and the garlic and cut into half. Trim, wash and peel the soupgreen and chop coarsely. Wash the tomato.

4 Add the vegetables and the bread to the roasting tin, pour over one third of the dark beer and reduce the heat to 350 °F. Roast the pork for 45 minutes, turn over and continue to roast for 30 minutes, basting frequently with the remaining beer and the roasting juices.

5 Remove the meat from the tin and place onto a grill, putting the roasting tin below to catch any juices. Roast the pork for 15 minutes until the meat is brown and crispy.

6 Strain the sauce through a fine colander and return to the roasting tin. Place the roasting tin on the cooker and bring the sauce to the boil.

7 Cut the pork into slices, place on warm plates and pour over the sauce. Serve with potato dumplings (see page 74) and cabbage salad with bacon (see page 61) or green salad.

Krautwickerl
Stuffed Cabbage with Ground Meat

Serves 4

1 medium-sized head cabbage

salt

2 stale hard bread rolls

3 onions

¼ bunch parsley

½ pound mixed ground meat (half pork, half beef)

2 eggs

freshly ground pepper

3 ½ ounces bacon

1 large carrot

3 ounces celeriac

1 clove garlic

2 tablespoons clarified butter

½ teaspoon ground cumin

½ teaspoon dried marjoram

freshly ground nutmeg

2 cups demi-glace (see page 121)

1 Remove the discolored leaves from the cabbage and cut off the stalk end. Bring 2 quarts of water to the boil in a large saucepan and add the cabbage. Cover and cook for 20 minutes.

2 Drain and rinse under cold water. Drain again. Remove 4 to 8 leaves from the head and flatten the center ribs with a knife. Cut 4 ounces of cabbage into fine strips.

3 Add the bread rolls (they must be hard and dry) to a small bowl, pour over some lukewarm water and allow to soak. Peel 1 onion and dice finely. Wash the parsley and shake dry. Pluck the leaves and chop finely.

4 With your hands, squeeze the bread rolls dry. Put them into a bowl, add the ground meat, the cabbage strips, the onion, the eggs and the parsley and mix well. Season with salt and pepper. Slice the bacon and set aside.

5 Peel the carrot, the celeriac, the remaining onion and the garlic and dice finely. Set aside.

6 Place some of the meat-mix on each leaf, turn in the ends and roll up. Secure with a toothpick. Heat the oven to 380 °F.

7 Melt the clarified butter in a roasting tin and fry the stuffed cabbage on both sides. Add the vegetables, the cumin, the marjoram and 1 pinch of nutmeg and fry briefly. Pour over the demi-glace, place the bacon on each stuffed cabbage and cover the roasting tin with a lid. Bake for 30 minutes.

8 Remove the stuffed cabbage and pour in some cornstarch dissolved in 1 tablespoon of water to thicken. Season with salt and pepper. Place the stuffed cabbage on warm plates and serve with mashed potatoes or boiled potatoes (see page 84).

Meat

Wiener Schnitzel
The Genuine Wiener Schnitzel

Serves 4

8 thin veal escalopes (¼ inch thick)

salt

freshly ground pepper

4 tablespoons of all-purpose flour

2 eggs

2 tablespoons milk

6 tablespoons breadcrumbs

6 tablespoons clarified butter

1 lemon

1 Wash the escalopes and dab dry. Place the escalopes between two sheets of cling film and pound them with a meat mallet until they are about ⅛ inch thick. Season with salt and pepper.

2 Spread the flour on one plate. Break the eggs into another plate, add the milk and whisk well. Spread the breadcrumbs on a third plate.

3 Roll the escalopes in the flour, shaking off excess flour. Then dip them into the egg-mix. Finally coat them in the breadcrumbs. Press in the breadcrumbs.

4 Melt the clarified butter in a large pan and fry the escalopes for 6 to 8 minutes on each side over medium heat until they are golden-brown.

5 Wash the lemon, rub dry and quarter. Place the escalopes on plates together with the lemon quarters and serve with potato salad or boiled potatoes sprinkled with parsley and a green salad.

Geschmorte Rinderroulade
Braised Beef Roulade with Bacon

Serves 4

4 onions

2 tablespoons butter

8 slices bacon

4 gherkins

4 large beef escalopes (7 ounces each)

salt

freshly ground pepper

2 tablespoons medium-hot mustard

4 tablespoons all-purpose flour

1 carrot

2 ounces celeriac

1 small leek

4 tablespoons clarified butter

1 tablespoon tomato paste

¾ cup red wine

2 cups demi-glace (see page 121)

1 bay leaf

dried thyme

allspice

1 Peel the onions, cut into half, then cut into fine half-moon shapes. Melt the butter in a pan. Fry the bacon and half of the onions until transparent. Set aside. Cut the gherkins lengthwise into slices.

2 Wash the escalopes and dab dry. Place the escalopes between two sheets of cling film and pound them softly with a meat mallet.

3 Season the escalopes with salt and pepper and spread the mustard over the meat. Place the fried onions, the bacon and the gherkins on the escalopes, turn in the ends and roll up. Secure with wooden skewers. Spread 2 tablespoons of flour on a plate and roll the stuffed escalopes in the flour.

4 Wash and peel the carrot and the celeriac, trim and wash the leek. Chop the vegetables coarsely.

5 Melt the clarified butter in a casserole and fry the escalopes until brown. Add the vegetables and fry briefly. Mix under the tomato paste and sprinkle with the remaining flour.

6 Pour over the red wine and the demi-glace. Add the bay leaf and season with 1 teaspoon of thyme and 1 pinch of allspice. Cover and allow to simmer for 60 to 90 minutes. After 45 minutes, turn over the escalopes.

7 Remove the escalopes from the sauce, set aside and keep warm. Strain the sauce through a fine colander and season with salt and pepper. Place the escalopes on plates and pour over the sauce. Serve with mashed potatoes and vegetables or a green salad.

Meat

Sauerbraten
Marinated Beef with Sliced Almonds

Serves 4

1 onion, 2 cloves

1 carrot, 1 parsley root

1 small leek

2 pounds beef (rump or top round roast of beef)

2 cups red wine vinegar

1 bay leaf

½ teaspoon black peppercorns

3 allspice

1 teaspoon dried thyme

½ bunch soupgreen (see page 98)

salt

freshly ground pepper

4 tablespoons clarified butter

2 tablespoons tomato paste

2 tablespoons all-purpose flour

¾ cup red wine

1 ½ cups demi-glace (see page 121)

3 tablespoons sliced almonds

1 Peel the onion and spike it with the cloves. Peel the carrot and the parsley root and cut into half. Trim and wash the leek and cut into half lenghtwise. Wash the meat and dab dry.

2 Add the vinegar, 2 cups of water, the vegetables and the spices to a bowl. Put the meat inside (it should be totally submerged). Cover and refrigerate. Allow the meat to marinate for at least 3 days, turning it occasionally.

3 Heat the oven to 325 °F. Trim, wash and peel the soupgreen and dice. Remove the meat from the marinade and dab dry. Season with salt and pepper. Strain the marinade through a fine colander. Reserve.

4 Melt the clarified butter in a roasting tin and fry the meat on all sides until brown. Add the vegetables and the tomato paste. Sprinkle the vegetables with the flour and fry briefly. Pour over 1 cup of the marinade, the red wine and the demi-glace. Cover the meat and allow to cook for 90 minutes on the middle rung of the oven. Turn the meat over once.

5 Remove the meat from the sauce, cover and keep warm. Strain the sauce through a fine colander and season with salt and pepper.

6 Cut the meat into slices and place on warm plates. Pour over the sauce and sprinkle with sliced almonds. Serve with red cabbage (see page 78) and home-made spaetzle.

Meat

Saures Kalbslüngerl
Sour Lung with Cream Sauce

Serves 4

For the meat:

2 pounds calves lung

1 bunch soupgreen (see page 98)

1 onion

salt

2 lemon slices

4 bay leaves

1 teaspoon peppercorns

½ teaspoon coriander seeds

3 cloves

½ cup red wine vinegar

½ cup red wine

For the cream sauce:

1 onion

4 tablespoons butter

3 tablespoons all-purpose flour

2 tablespoons lemon juice

½ bunch parsley

¾ cup cream

salt, freshly ground pepper

1 To prepare the meat, wash the lung and drain. Trim, peel and wash the soupgreen and dice. Peel the onion and quarter.

2 Bring 2 quarts of salted water to the boil in a large saucepan and add the lung, the vegetables, the lemon slices and the spices. Bring to the boil, cover and allow to simmer for 45 minutes.

3 Remove the meat from the marinade. Place it under a heavy cutting board, put some weights on top and allow to cool.

4 Cut the cold lung into thin strips. Strain the marinade through a sieve and add the vinegar and the wine. Put the meat into a bowl and cover with the marinade. Refrigerate and allow to marinate for at least 8 hours.

5 To prepare the sauce, drain the meat and reserve the marinade. Peel the onion and dice finely. Melt the butter in a pan and fry the onions until transparent. Sprinkle the onions with the flour and fry until golden-brown. Pour over 3 cups of the marinade and bring to the boil, stirring constantly.

6 Add the strips of lung to the sauce, pour over the lemon juice and bring to the boil. Allow to simmer for 10 minutes.

7 Wash the parsley and shake dry. Pluck the leaves and chop finely. Add the cream to the sauce and season with salt and pepper. Serve the strips of lung with bread dumplings in soup plates sprinkled with parsley.

Meat

Kalbsbrust
Stuffed Breast of Veal

Serves 4

2 stale hard bread rolls

½ cup lukewarm milk

2 carrots

2 onions

2 ounces bacon

½ bunch parsley

1 tablespoon butter

4 ½ pounds breast of veal (bones and inner skin removed to get a pocket)

salt

freshly ground pepper

paprika

2 eggs

1 tablespoon breadcrumbs

freshly ground nutmeg

2 tablespoons clarified butter

½ cup dry white wine

1 ½ cup beef consommé (see page 52)

1 teaspoon cornstarch

1 To prepare the stuffing, cut the bread rolls (they must be hard and dry) into thin slices, add to a bowl, pour over the lukewarm milk and allow to soak.

2 Peel the onions. Dice 1 onion finely, cut the other onion in half. Peel the carrots. Dice 1 carrot finely, cut the other in half lengthwise. Dice the bacon into small cubes. Wash the parsley, shake dry, pluck the leaves and chop finely.

3 Melt the butter in a pan and fry the bacon, the diced onion and the diced carrot. With your hands squeeze the bread dry, add to the pan, sprinkle with the parsley and fry briefly. Remove from the heat and allow to cool.

4 Wash the breast of veal, also on the inside, and dab dry. Season with salt, pepper and paprika, inside and outside. Heat the oven to 350 °F.

5 Add the eggs and the breadcrumbs to the stuffing-mix. Season with salt, pepper and 1 pinch of nutmeg and mix well. Carefully fill the stuffing into the pocket and sew up with a strong thread.

6 Melt the clarified butter in a roasting tin and fry the breast of veal on all sides until brown. Add the halved onion and the halved carrot and pour over the white wine and the consommé. Cover and cook in the oven for 90 minutes, basting frequently with the roasting juices so that the meat does not turn dry.

7 Remove the meat, cover and keep warm. Strain the sauce through a sieve and pour in the cornstarch dissolved in 1 tablespoon of cold water to thicken. Cut the stuffed breast of veal into 1 inch thick slices and serve with either potato salad or boiled potatoes sprinkled with parsley and a salad.

Pichelsteiner Eintopf
Pichelsteiner Stew

Serves 4

½ pound veal

½ pound beef

½ pound pork (from the shoulder)

2 ounces bone marrow

2 onions

1 pound Savoy cabbage

4 ounces celeriac

⅔ pound carrots

1 pound waxy potatoes

2 tablespoons oil

salt

freshly ground pepper

3 cups beef consommé (see page 52)

1 bunch parsley

1 Wash the meat, dab dry and dice into thumb-sized cubes.

2 Peel the onions, cut into half, then cut into fine half-moon shapes. Trim and wash the Savoy cabbage, quarter and cut into strips. Peel the celeriac and dice finely.

3 Peel the carrots and the potatoes and cut into thick slices.

4 Heat the oil in a pan, fry the onions until transparent, then fry the meat until brown. Season with salt and pepper. Bring the beef consommé to the boil in a saucepan.

5 Pile meat, vegetables and potatoes layer by layer into a saucepan, using the marrow for the bottom layer and the top layer, and pour over the beef consommé. Allow to simmer for 60 minutes without stirring. Check if there is enough liquid in the saucepan. If necessary, pour over more consommé.

6 Wash the parsley, shake dry, pluck the leaves and chop finely. Season the stew with salt and pepper. Serve sprinkled with parsley or marjoram and serve with rye bread.

Meat

Böfflamott
Bavarian Boeuf à la Mode

Serves 4

1 onion

1 bunch soupgreen (see page 98)

1 1/2 pound beef (rump roast)

2/3 cup red wine vinegar

2/3 cup red wine

3 peppercorns

1 sprig of thyme

1 bay leaf

1 large carrot

3 ounces celeriac

1 small leek

1/2 calf's foot

salt

freshly ground pepper

3 tablespoons clarified butter

1 Peel the onion and dice finely. Trim, wash and peel the soupgreen and dice finely. Wash the beef, dab dry and put into a bowl with all the vegetables.

2 Bring the vinegar, the red wine and 3 cups of water to the boil. Grind the peppercorns with a mortar. Wash the thyme and shake dry. Add the bay leaf and the spices to the boiling marinade. Allow to cool. When cold, pour over the meat and the vegetables. Cover and keep refrigerated. Allow the meat to marinade for 3 to 4 days.

3 Peel the carrot and the celeriac, trim and wash the leek. Dice the vegetables finely.

4 Remove the meat from the marinade, dab dry and season with salt and pepper. Melt the clarified butter in a saucepan and fry the meat on all sides until brown. Strain the marinade through a sieve.

5 Add the vegetables to the meat and fry. Pour over half of the marinade and simmer the Böfflamott for 2 to 3 hours, continuously adding more marinade.

6 Remove the meat and wrap in metal foil. Remove the bay leaf. Blend or process the juices and the vegetables until smooth. Strain the sauce through a fine colander and reduce by half over high heat. Cut the meat into slices, pour over the sauce and serve with either potato dumplings or bread dumplings (see page 74 and 68).

Tellerfleisch
Braised Beef with Horseradish

Serves 4

1 ½ pounds beef (rump roast)

1 bunch soupgreen (see page 98)

1 clove garlic

salt

freshly ground pepper

1 carrot

3 ounces celeriac

3 ounces leek

1 bunch chives

3 inches of horseradish

1 Wash the meat and dab dry. Trim, wash and peel the soupgreen and dice finely. Peel the garlic.

2 Bring 1 ½ quarts of water to the boil in a large saucepan. Add a heaped teaspoon of salt and some pepper. Put the meat into the boiling water and simmer for 30 minutes. Skim off the scum with a slotted ladle.

3 Add the soupgreen and the garlic, cover and continue to simmer for 60 minutes.

4 Peel the carrot and the celeriac, trim and wash the leek. Cut the vegetables into fine strips.

5 Remove the meat from the consommé, cover and keep warm. Strain the consommé through a sieve, add the vegetables strips and cook until soft.

6 Wash the chives, shake dry and cut into fine rolls. Peel the horseradish and grate finely.

7 Cut the meat into slices, place on warm soup plates and pour over some consommé. Add the vegetables and sprinkle with chives. Serve with freshly grated horseradish and boiled potatoes (see page 84).

Hofbräu-Bierkutschergulasch
Beer Goulash with Cabbage

Serves 4

1 1/2 pounds pork (from the shoulder)

1 clove garlic

1/2 teaspoon cumin

1/2 teaspoon dried marjoram

1/2 quart lager beer

2 large onions

4 tablespoons clarified butter

4 tablespoons tomato paste

1 1/2 cups demi-glace (see page 121)

1/2 pound cabbage

2 tablespoons cornstarch

salt

freshly ground pepper

sugar

1 tablespoon lemon juice

1 Wash the meat and dab dry. Dice the meat into cubes and put into a bowl. Peel the garlic and cut into half. Add the garlic and the spices to the meat and pour over the beer. Cover and keep refrigerated. Allow the meat to marinate over night.

2 Remove the meat from the marinade. Reserve the marinade. Peel the onion and cut into fine strips.

3 Melt the clarified butter in a pan and fry the meat until brown, stirring constantly. Add the onion and the tomato paste and fry briefly.

4 Pour the marinade and the demi-glace over the meat, cover and allow to simmer for 60 minutes.

5 Remove the discolored leaves from the cabbage and cut the leaves into small diamond shapes. 20 minutes before the meat is tender, add the cabbage diamonds to the goulash.

6 Dissolve the cornstarch in 1 tablespoon of cold water and add to the goulash to thicken.

7 Season the goulash with salt and pepper, 1 pinch of sugar and lemon juice and serve with bread dumplings and a green salad.

Meat

Geschmorte Lammhaxe
Braised Lamb Knuckle

Serves 4

4 lamb knuckles
freshly ground pepper
4 cloves garlic
2 carrots
1 small celeriac
1 red bell pepper
1 green bell pepper
3 ounces clarified butter
2 cups red wine
2 ¼ cups good veal stock
1 tablespoon cornstarch

1 Wash the lamb knuckles and dab dry. Season with salt and pepper. Peel the garlic and dice finely.

2 Peel the carrots and the celeriac and dice finely. Cut the peppers in half lengthwise, de-seed, wash and dice finely.

3 Melt half of the clarified butter in a pan and fry the vegetables, stirring constantly. Heat the oven to 410 °F.

4 Melt the remaining clarified butter in a roasting tin and fry the knuckles on all sides until brown. Add the garlic and fry briefly. Pour over the red wine and the veal stock, add the fried vegetables, cover and allow to cook for 60 minutes.

5 Remove the meat from the sauce, cover and keep warm. Season the sauce with salt and pepper. Pour over some cornstarch dissolved in 1 tablespoon of cold water to thicken.

6 Place the knuckles on warm plates and serve with haricot beans and boiled potatoes (see page 84).

Meat

Hausgemachte braune Kraftsauce
Home-Made Demi-Glace

Makes about 1 quart

2 1/2 pounds veal and pork bones

1/4 pound bacon

1 onion, 1 clove garlic, 1 carrot, 1 parsley root

3 ounces celeriac

1 small leek

3 tablespoons clarified butter

2 tablespoons tomato paste

2 tablespoons all-purpose flour

paprika

1 1/2 cups red wine

2 quarts beef consommé (see page 52)

1 bay leaf, dried thyme, allspice, salt, freshly ground pepper

1 Wash the bones and dab dry. Dice the bacon into small cubes. Peel the onion, the garlic, the carrot, the parsley root and the celeriac, trim and wash the leek. Dice the vegetables finely.

2 Melt the clarified butter in a pan and fry the bacon. Add the bones. Add the diced vegetables and fry briefly.

3 Mix under the tomato paste, stirring constantly until it turns brown. Sprinkle with flour and 1 pinch of paprika. Pour over the red wine and the consommé.

4 Add the bay leaf, 1/2 teaspoon of thyme, 1/2 teaspoon of allspice and season with salt and pepper. Allow the sauce to simmer for 3 to 4 hours, stirring occasionally.

5 Strain the sauce through a sieve. Season with salt and pepper. Allow to cool. Skim the fat from the sauce.

Our chef suggests:

Pour the sauce into ice cube trays and store in the freezer. The sauce can be used to enrich other dark sauces, for roasts and fried meat.

Desserts

When it comes to desserts, the Bavarians tend to get on very well with their Austrian neighbors. Steamed dumplings, Applestrudel or the Emperor's Pancakes are popular desserts that will make people go weak at the knees on this side of the Alps, too.

Kaiserschmarrn
The Emperor's Pancakes with Apple Mousse

Serves 4

For the pancakes:

3 ounces raisins

2 tablespoons dark rum

6 eggs

½ pound all-purpose flour

2 cups milk

2 tablespoons vanilla extract

3 tablespoons sugar

salt

2 tablespoons vegetable oil

5 tablespoons unsalted butter

2 ounces confectioner's sugar

For the apple mousse:

5 apples

grated rind of ½ lemon

juice of 1 lemon

1 cinnamon stick

5 tablespoons sugar

1 Soak the raisins in rum over night.

2 For the apple mousse, wash and quarter the apples (do not peel them). Put them into a saucepan. Add the lemon rind and the cinnamon stick. Pour over the lemon juice and enough water to cover the apples. Cook the apples until soft.

3 Strain the apples through a fine colander into a bowl and add half of the sugar. Allow to cool, while adding the remaining sugar.

4 Separate the eggs. Put the egg whites into a tall mixing bowl and set aside. Sift the flour into a bowl. Add the egg yolks, the milk and the vanilla extract and mix a batter. Whisk the egg whites with the sugar and 1 pinch of salt until they hold stiff peaks. Fold the egg whites into the batter. Heat the oven grill.

5 Grease two ovenproof dishes with the oil and pour in the batter, 1 ½ inch deep. Sprinkle with the raisins and bake the pancakes in the oven until golden on one side.

6 Turn the pancakes over and place the dishes into the oven. Bake the pancakes for 3 minutes on each side under the grill until golden-brown. Take the dishes out of the oven and with two forks tear the pancakes into bite-sized pieces.

7 Add the butter and sprinkle with half of the confectioner's sugar. Put the pancakes back into the oven until the sugar has caramelized.

8 Place the pancakes on plates, sprinkle with the remaining confectioner's sugar and serve with apple mousse.

Desserts

Hofbräu-Biereis
Ice Cream with Lime and Beer

Serves 4
2 1/2 cups cream
2/3 cup milk
salt
6 egg yolks
6 tablespoons sugar
2/3 cup lager beer
1 teaspoon lime juice
1/2 teaspoon of grated lime rind

1 Heat the cream, the milk and 1 pinch of salt in a saucepan but do not boil.

2 Whisk the egg yolks and the sugar in a metal bowl until creamy.

3 Set the bowl over hot water, pour in the cream-milk and whisk over medium heat until the mixture thickens enough to coat the back of a spoon.

4 Set the bowl over an ice bath and beat to cool the mixture. Pour in the beer and the lime juice, add the lime rind and stir. Allow to stand for 5 minutes, then strain through a sieve. Chill an ice cream container in the freezer.

5 Process the mixture in an ice cream machine according to manufacturer's instructions. Put the ice cream into the chilled container and cover. Keep in the freezer for 2 hours before serving.

Our chef suggests:

If you do not have an ice cream machine, put the mixture into the freezer for 60 minutes, stirring it regularly so that it turns creamy. Keep in the freezer for 2 hours before serving.

Desserts

Dampfnudeln
Steamed Yeast Dumplings with Vanilla Custard Sauce

Serves 4

1 pound all-purpose flour
2 tablespoons sugar
2 ½ teaspoons active dry yeast
½ quart milk
4 ounces unsalted butter
1-2 eggs
grated rind of ½ lemon
salt
flour

1 Sift the flour into a bowl and mix in 1 teaspoon of sugar and the yeast. Warm half of the milk in a saucepan. Add 4 tablespoons of butter and allow to melt. Fold the eggs, the lemon rind and 1 pinch of salt into the milk and add to the flour.

2 Vigorously beat the dough for 5 minutes until it forms bubbles, then cover, and in a warm spot, allow to rest for 60 minutes until it has doubled in size.

3 With floured hands, shape the dough into 8 fist-sized dumplings. Cover and let them rest for 30 minutes.

4 In a wide pot, melt the remaining butter, the remaining sugar and 1 pinch of salt. Pour in the remaining milk. Add the dumplings, arranged in one layer, touching each other.

5 Cover the pot and additionally seal the edges – where the lid rests on the pot – with a damp cloth in order to keep the steam inside. Bring the milk to a boil, then reduce the heat and steam the dumplings over low heat for 30 minutes. Do not open the lid or the dumplings will collapse.

6 Remove from the heat and allow the dumplings to stand for a few minutes.

7 Remove the lid and carefully lift the dumplings out of the pot. Place on dessert plates. Sprinkle with sugar and ground cinnamon and serve with vanilla custard sauce (see page 133).

Desserts

Apfelkücherl
Apple Pancakes

Serves 4

½ pound all-purpose flour

salt

1 ½ cups lager beer

(alternatively, you can use white wine or sparkling mineral water)

1 tablespoon vegetable oil

3 tablespoons sugar

3 eggs

4-5 apples

5 tablespoons confectioner's sugar

1 teaspoon ground cinnamon

juice of one lemon

2 tablespoons dark rum

2 cups vegetable oil, for frying

1 For the batter, sift the flour into a bowl and add 1 pinch of salt. Pour in the beer and 1 tablespoon of oil and add the sugar. Separate the eggs. Put the egg whites into a tall mixing bowl and set aside. Add the egg yolks to the batter and beat well. Allow the batter to rest for 20 minutes in the refrigerator.

2 Whisk the egg whites until they hold stiff peaks and fold into the batter.

3 Peel the apples, core and cut into ½ inch rings.

4 Mix the confectioner's sugar and the cinnamon. Place the apple rings into a bowl, sprinkle with lemon juice, rum and half of the cinnamon-sugar. Allow to stand briefly.

5 In a pan, heat 1 ½ inch of oil. Dip the apple rings into the batter and bake them in the hot oil until they are golden. Turn them over and remove them with a slotted ladle. Drain on kitchen paper.

6 White still hot, sprinkle the apple pancakes with the remaining cinnamon-sugar and serve immediately.

Desserts

Zwetschgendatschi
Plum Cake with Crumble

For the dough:
1 pound all-purpose flour
3 teaspoons active dry yeast
2 ounces sugar
2 1/4 cup milk
4 tablespoons soft unsalted butter
2 eggs
salt

For the plum topping:
2 1/2 pounds plums
3/4 pound all-purpose flour
5 ounces sugar
1 teaspoon ground cinnamon
salt
1/4 pound or 1/2 cup unsalted butter

1 For the pastry, sift the flour into a bowl. Mix in 1 teaspoon of sugar and the yeast. Warm the milk in a saucepan. Add the butter and allow to melt. Fold the eggs and 1 pinch of salt into the milk and add to the flour.

2 Vigorously beat the dough for 5 minutes until it forms bubbles, then cover, and in a warm spot, allow to rest for 60 minutes until it has doubled in size.

3 For the topping, wash the plums and dab dry. Cut into half and pit, making a small cut in the narrow end of each plum half. Heat the oven to 350 °F.

4 Line a baking tray with baking paper. Knead the dough once more, roll it out and place it on the baking tray, forming a little rim. Lay the plums cut-side up on the dough in an overlapping fashion.

5 To make the crumble topping, sift the flour into a bowl. Add the sugar, the cinnamon and 1 pinch of salt. Melt the butter in a pan and add to the flour, stirring constantly. Use the dough hook of a hand mixer to process the ingredients until they have the consistency of coarse breadcrumbs. Sprinkle the crumbles evenly over the plums.

6 Bake the plum cake on the middle rung of the oven for 40 minutes until golden-brown. Remove from the oven, allow to cool slightly and cut into squares. Serve with whipped cream.

Desserts

Bayerisch Creme
Bavarian Cream (Crème Bavaroise)

Serves 4

1 3/4 cups cream

3/4 ounce gelatin

1 cup milk

half a vanilla pod

3 egg yolks

3 tablespoons sugar

salt

1/4 cup Framboise (alternatively, you can use Kirsch or Grand Marnier)

1 Whip the cream until it holds stiff peaks. Set aside and keep refrigerated. Mix the gelatin with 1 tablespoon of cold water.

2 Bring the milk and the scraped inside of the vanilla pod just to the boil.

3 Whisk the egg yolks with 1 pinch of salt in a metal bowl until creamy. Carefully pour the hot vanilla milk through a sieve into the egg yolks, stirring constantly. Set the bowl over hot water and whisk until the mixture thickens enough to coat the back of a spoon.

4 Add the gelatin to the crème and pour in the Framboise. Place the crème over an ice bath and stir to cool.

5 Shortly before the crème begins to set, fold in the whipped cream. Pour the crème into a bowl and keep refrigerated for 2 hours.

6 Remove the crème from the fridge. With two spoons, scoop the crème onto dessert plates. Garnish with fresh raspberries or red currants.

Desserts

Apfelstrudel
Applestrudel with Cream Topping

Serves 4

For the pastry:

1/2 pound all-purpose flour

salt

2 1/2 tablespoons vegetable oil

For the filling:

2 pounds tart apples

juice of 1 lemon

1 teaspoon grated lemon rind

4 ounces sugar

1/2 teaspoon ground cinnamon

2 tablespoons dark rum

2 ounces raisins

2 ounces coarsely chopped hazelnuts

3 tablespoons unsalted butter

4 tablespoons breadcrumbs

For the cream topping:

1/2 cup milk

1/2 cup cream

2 tablespoons unsalted butter

1 For the pastry, sift the flour into a bowl. Add 3/4 cup of warm water, 2 tablespoons of oil and one pinch of salt. Knead until smooth. Brush with the remaining oil and allow the pastry to rest for at least 30 minutes.

2 For the filling, peel, quarter and core the apples. Cut into thin slices. Put the apple slices into a bowl and sprinkle with lemon juice. Add the lemon rind, sugar, ground cinnamon, rum, raisins and nuts and mix well.

3 Melt 1 tablespoon of butter in a pan and fry the breadcrumbs until golden. Heat the oven to 375 °F. Brush a baking tin with butter.

4 Spread a clean kitchen towel over the work surface, flour it and place the pastry on it. First, spread the pastry with a rolling pin. Then flour your hands and put them with the backs up under the pastry. Start to stretch the pastry in all directions. Ultimately, the pastry has to be as thin as a sheet.

5 Brush the pastry with the remaining melted butter. Cover with the apple filling and the fried breadcrumbs, leaving a 3-inch border free. Fold in two sides. To roll up the strudel, take two corners of the towel and lift them a little, so that the strudel starts rolling up. Proceed until it is rolled up. Depending on the size of the baking tin, cut the strudel into 2 or 3 pieces and place them alongside each other into the tin. Bake in the preheated oven for 25 minutes.

6 For the topping, heat the milk, cream and butter in a pan. Remove the strudel from the oven and pour over the topping. Return the strudel to the oven and bake for 30 minutes.

7 Remove the strudel from the oven and sprinkle with some confectioner's sugar. Cut the strudel into thick slices and serve it hot or cold with vanilla custard sauce (see page 133).

Desserts

Vanillesauce
Vanilla Custard Sauce with Dark Rum

Serves 4:
½ vanilla pod
2 ¼ cups cream
2 ¼ cups milk
4 tablespoons sugar
2 eggs
2 teaspoons cornstarch
1 tablespoon dark rum

1 Cut the vanilla pod lengthwise without cutting it all the way through. With a sharp knife, scrape the inside and put both the pod and the pulp into a pan. Pour in the cream and 2 cups of milk and bring just to the boil. Dissolve half of the sugar in the cream-milk. Remove the vanilla pod and strain the mixture through a fine sieve.

2 Separate the eggs. Whisk the egg yolks with the remaining milk, the cornstarch and the remaining sugar and pour into the hot vanilla milk. Bring just to the boil and pour in the rum. Remove from the heat.

3 Whisk the egg whites until they hold stiff peaks. Fold the egg whites into the hot custard sauce. You can also add some whipped cream. Serve the vanilla custard sauce either hot or chilled.

Our chef suggests:

*If vanilla pods are not available,
you can use 1 teaspoon vanilla extract or
1 teaspoon ground vanilla pods instead.*

Index of Recipes

A

Apple Lard Dripping on Fresh Rye Bread *(Apfelgriebenschmalz auf frischem Bauernbrot)* 39
Apple Pancakes *(Apfelkücherl im Bierteig)* 128
Applestrudel with Cream Topping *(Apfelstrudel mit Rahmguss)* 132
Asparagus Crepes au Gratin *(Pfannkuchen, überbackene)* 67

B

Bavarian Cream *(Bayerisch Creme mit Himbeergeist)* 130
Beef Aspic with Crème Fraîche *(Tafelspitzsülze)* 42
Beef Consommé *(Klare Rinderbrühe)* 52
Beef Consommé with Grits Dumplings *(Grießnockerlsuppe)* 56
Beef Consommé with Liver Dumplings and Fresh Marjoram *(Leberknödelsuppe)* 57
Beef Consommé with Strips of Crepes *(Pfannkuchensuppe)* 58
Beef Roulade, Braised, with Bacon *(Geschmorte Rinderroulade)* 108
Beef Salad with White Mushrooms *(Rindfleischsalat)* 49
Beer Goulash with Cabbage *(Hofbräu-Bierkutschergulasch)* 118
Beetroot Salad with Yogurt Dressing *(Rote-Bete-Salat)* 63
Bœuf à la Mode, Bavarian *(Böfflamott)* 116
Braised Beef with Horseradish *(Tellerfleisch)* 117
Braised Lamb Knuckle *(Lammhaxe, geschmorte)* 120
Bread Dumplings *(Semmelknödel)* 68
Breast of Veal, Stuffed, *(Kalbsbrust)* 112
Brewmaster's Pork Steak with Baked Potatoes *(Braumeistersteak)* 103

C

Cabbage Salad with Bacon *(Krautsalat)* 61
Cabbage, Bavarian, with Bacon *(Bayerisch Kraut mit Speck)* 79
Chicken Breasts, Browned, on Tomato Noodles *(Hähnchenbrustfilet)* 95
Cream Cheese with Herbs Served in Red Pepper *(Kräuterfrischkäse)* 46
Crème Bavaroise *(Bayrisch Creme)* 130

D

Dark Beer Sauce *(Dunkelbiersauce)* 104
Demi-Glace, Home-Made, *(Kraftsauce, hausgemachte braune)* 121
Duck à l'Orange, Roast *(Gebratene Ente)* 96

E

Emperor's Pancakes, The, with Apple Mousse *(Kaiserschmarrn)* 124

F

Finger Noodles with Sauerkraut *(Schupfnudeln)* 76
Fish Fritters with Breadcrumb Crust *(Fischpflanzerl)* 89
Fried Potatoes with Onions *(Röstkartoffeln)* 70

G

Goose Giblets in White Wine Sauce *(Gänseklein)* 98
Goulash Soup with Diced Potatoes *(Gulaschsuppe)* 54
Grits Dumplings *(Grießnockerl)* 56

H

Hofbräu Beer Goulasch with Cabbage *(Hofbräu-Bierkutschergulasch)* 118
Home-made Demi-Glace *(hausgemachte braune Kraftsauce)* 121

I

Ice Cream with Lime and Beer *(Hofbräu-Biereis)* 125

L

Lamb Knuckle, Braised *(Geschmorte Lammhaxe)* 120
Liver Dumplings *(Leberknödel)* 57

M

Marinated Beef with Sliced Almonds *(Sauerbraten)* 110

Munich Sausage Salad with Onion Rings *(Münchner Wurstsalat)* 48

Mushrooms in Cream Sauce with Bread Dumplings *(Gemischte Schwammerl)* 68

O

Obatzda with Chives and Onion Rings *(Obatzda)* 38

Original Munich Potato Dumplings *(Reiberknödel)* 74

P

Pichelsteiner Stew *(Pichelsteiner Eintopf)* 114

Pikeperch with Sauce Hollandaise *(Gebratener Zander)* 90

Plum Cake with Crumble *(Zwetschgendatschi)* 129

Pork Kidneys with Gherkins *(Saure Schweinenierchen)* 102

Pork Knuckle with Potato Dumpling and Cabbage Salad *(Schweinshaxe)* 100

Pork Steak, Brewmaster's, with Baked Potatoes *(Braumeistersteak)* 103

Potato Dumplings, Original Munich, with Nutmeg *(Reiberknödel)* 74

Potato Fritters with Cumin *(Kaspressknödel)* 72

Potato Salad with Cucumber *(Kartoffelsalat)* 62

Potato Soup, Bavarian, with Bacon *(Kartoffelsuppe mit Speck)* 53

Potato Spread with Sour Cream *(Kartoffelkas)* 43

R

Radish Salad with Watercress *(Rettichsalat)* 60

Radishes, Fresh, with Chives on Bread *(Frischer Radi)* 40

Red Cabbage with Apples *(Blaukraut mit Äpfeln)* 78

Roast Chicken with Potato Salad *(Wiesnhendl)* 94

Roast Duck à l'Orange *(Gebratene Ente)* 96

Roast Pork with Dark Beer Sauce *(Schweinebraten)* 104

Rosefish with Vegetable Juliennes and White Wine Sauce *(Gedünstetes Rotbarschfilet)* 82

S

Sauerkraut with Five Spices *(Sauerkraut)* 75

Savoy Cabbage Fritters with Salmon Sauce *(Wirsingpflanzerl)* 86

Shredded Potatoes with Sour Cream *(Kartoffelschmarrn)* 71

Smoked Fish Mousse with Lettuce *(Räucherfischmousse)* 45

Smoked Trout Fillet with Horseradish *(Geräuchertes Forellenfilet)* 44

Sole Roulades with Swiss Chard and Tomato Sauce *(Seezungenrouladen)* 88

Sour Lung with Cream Sauce *(Saures Kalbslüngerl)* 111

Spaetzle with Emmental Cheese and Fried Onion Rings *(Kasspatzen, Allgäuer)* 66

Stew »Pichelsteiner« *(Eintopf, Pichelsteiner)* 114

Stuffed Cabbage with Ground Meat *(Krautwickerl)* 106

T

The Genuine Wiener Schnitzel *(Wiener Schnitzel)* 107

Trout »Müllerin Art« *(Forelle »Müllerin Art«)* 84

Trout au Bleu *(Forelle »blau«)* 83

Trout Fillets, Smoked, with Horseradish *(Forellenfilet, geräuchertes)* 44

Turkey Ragout with Mushrooms *(Putengeschnetzeltes)* 99

V

Vanilla Custard Sauce with Dark Rum *(Vanillesauce)* 133

W

Wiener Schnitzel *(Wiener Schnitzel)* 107

Y

Yeast Dumplings, Steamed, with Vanilla Custard Sauce *(Dampfnudeln mit Vanillesauce)* 126

The Hofbräu-Hymn

In München is the Hofbräuhaus, eins, zwei, gsuffa,
Where the kegs are overflowing, eins, zwei, gsuffa,
There is always some brave man, eins, zwei, gsuffa,
Who wants to show how much he can drink, eins, zwei, gsuffa.
You find him starting early in the morning,
And coming home late at night – Ah, the beautiful Hofbräuhaus.

Acknowledgements

Illustration credits:
Front cover illustration: Rupert Stöckl. Back cover photos: Tobias Ranzinger (top left); Kai Stiepel (top right and bottom). AKG-Images: p. 15 (top and bottom); Archive Hofbräuhaus Munich, Familie Sperger: p. 4, 23 (left and right), 25, 33 (top); Stefan Braun: p. 13; Dr. Kai-Uwe Nielsen: p. 6, 12 (bottom left and top), 14, 17 (left), 18, 19 (left and right), 20, 21 (left and right), 22, 24, 26–27, 28, 29 (from left to right), 30, 32, 33 (bottom), 34; Tobias Ranzinger: p. 8–9, 11, 17 (right);

Kai Stiepel: p. 36–37, 41, 47, 50–51, 55, 59, 64–65, 69, 73, 77, 80–81, 85, 87, 91, 92–93, 97, 101, 105, 109, 113, 115, 119, 122–123, 127, 131; Kuni Taguchi: p. 10; Stilla Weiß: p. 35
Frank Duffek: all festoons and food drawings: p. 30, 31, 44, 48, 56, 62, 75, 78, 89, 107, 128.

Citation
»In München steht ein Hofbräuhaus ...«, above:
© Wilhelm Gebauer Leipzig. By courtesy of
W. Gebauer Musikverlag Wiesbaden.